DEIRDRE

A LIFE ON
CORONATION STREET

GLENDA YOUNG

1 3 5 7 9 10 8 6 4 2

CENTURY

20 Vauxhall Bridge Road
London SW1V 2SA

Century is part of the Penguin Random House group of
companies whose addresses can be found at
global.penguinrandomhouse.com

Coronation Street is an **ITV Studios Production**

Written by
Glenda Young

Glenda Young has asserted her right to be identified
as the author of this Work in accordance with
the Copyright, Designs and Patents Act 1988

Design
Tim Barnes ℞ **chicken**
herechickychicky.com

Picture research
Janice Troup
Dave Woodward

Coronation Street images courtesy
ITV Studios Ltd
except p.200 **McPix Ltd/Rex Shutter Stock**

Background and stock images
www.shutterstock.com

Every reasonable effort has been made to contact all
copyright holders, but if there are any errors or omissions,
we will insert the appropriate acknowledgment in
subsequent printings of this book.

First published by **Century** in 2015

www.randomhouse.co.uk

A CIP catalogue record for this book
is available from the British Library.

ISBN **978 1 7808 9489 8**

Printed and bound in India by
Replika Press Pvt Ltd

Penguin Random House is committed
to a sustainable future for our business, our readers
and our planet. This book is made from
Forest Stewardship Council® certified paper.

Contents

Introduction

SINCE HER FIRST APPEARANCE ON *CORONATION STREET* IN 1972, Deirdre Barlow has been involved in some of the most exciting and dramatic storylines in the history of the show. She quickly became one of the most enduring and best loved characters.

She started life on *Coronation Street* as a vivacious teenager and we have watched over the years as life took its toll on her, turning her into a weary woman of the world.

Deirdre was someone who was constantly trying to improve her lot. Her life was filled with tears and traumas and she was never far away from a crisis. She struggled to look after her family and always thought that the grass was greener on the other side, with another man.

This amazing fictional character has been through numerous affairs and sensational storylines. She's been imprisoned, twice driven to the brink of suicide; she's had three husbands, four weddings – and countless pairs of specs.

Deirdre brought sex appeal to *Coronation Street*. She joined a long line of feisty females and didn't have long to wait for love to come calling.

She soon became a firm favourite, turning into one of the most popular characters, who starred in some of the defining moments of British TV. She was one of the first single mums in a soap and was almost written out when her on-screen husband left the show.

Soap characters are lucky if they are at the heart of one huge storyline. Deirdre had that luck twice, with her love triangle storyline making the leap from screen to headline news for the first time in British soap. She would do it again with her prison sentence.

Deirdre's storylines have followed highs and lows, love and betrayal, slaps, snogs, kisses and tears. She was one of *Coronation Street*'s best-loved women, held in high affection by fans around the world, and this is her story.

Deirdre's
TOP 10 STORYLINES

#1 **1998** **FREE THE WEATHERFIELD ONE** 〈 119 〉

DEIRDRE FELL FOR FAKE PILOT JON LINDSAY AND ENDED UP IN COURT on a fraud trial. Jon was a con man of the highest order and gullible Deirdre believed all of his lies. In court, Deirdre was sent down for eighteen months. As the judge gave his sentence, Deirdre broke down and cried: **'I didn't do any of it!'**

Deirdre's storyline resulted in a huge public response. The campaign to Free the Weatherfield One was launched. Headlines screamed against the injustice of her sentence and questions were asked in Parliament. Deirdre was freed after just three weeks in jail.

#2 **1983** **LOVE TRIANGLE WITH KEN AND MIKE** 〈 63 〉

Deirdre torn between Ken and Mike

OVER 18 MILLION FANS TUNED IN TO WATCH THE LOVE TRIANGLE OF Deirdre, Ken and Mike. It was the most emotionally gripping storyline that *Coronation Street* had ever run. It resulted in unprecedented reaction from the public and the press. Deirdre and Ken split for the first time and although they would end up together again, their marriage would never truly recover.

#3 1981/2005 **TWO WEDDINGS TO KEN** ⟨ 56 ⟩⟨ 148 ⟩

WHEN DEIRDRE MARRIED KEN FOR THE FIRST TIME IN 1981 IT CEMENTED their partnership as one of the best-loved couples on television. More than 15 million viewers tuned in to watch their first wedding in 1981. It took place two days before HRH Prince Charles married Lady Diana Spencer.

Their 2005 wedding coincided almost exactly with HRH Prince Charles's wedding to Camilla Parker Bowles. The Barlows beat the royals in the ratings. More than 13 million viewers tuned in to celebrate Ken and Deirdre tying the knot for a second time, compared to 8 million viewers for the royal wedding.

#4 1979 **LORRY CRASHES INTO THE ROVERS** ⟨ 42 ⟩

DEIRDRE WAS AT THE HEART OF ONE OF CORONATION STREET'S MOST gripping storylines when a lorry crashed into the Rovers. The disaster saw Deirdre brought to the brink of desperation as she considered suicide when Tracy was kidnapped in the crash.

 #5   2010   **GAIL PIES DEIRDRE**   ⟨176⟩

DEIRDRE WAS CAUGHT KISSING LEWIS ARCHER – THEIR SNOG WAS
recorded on CCTV at Barlow's Bookies. The kiss was given a very public airing when
it was shown at Gail's house, which was full of people attending Audrey's leaving
party. Furious with Deirdre for making a mockery of her mother, Gail picked up a
Manchester tart filled with cream and chucked it at Deirdre. It hit Deirdre slap-bang
in the middle of her face. The cream stuck to Deirdre's glasses. **'Ken! Do something!'**
she wailed.

 #6   2007   **DEIRDRE AND TRACY STAR IN TWO-HANDER** ⟨160⟩

THERE HAVE ONLY EVER BEEN TWO *CORONATION STREET* EPISODES
featuring just two characters. One of those was a tense two-hander when Tracy
confessed to Deirdre that she'd killed Charlie Stubbs. The episode was set in Deirdre's
house as she sat drinking wine and smoking while Tracy did the ironing. Deirdre's
relationship with Tracy came under the spotlight in the two-hander. Old wounds were
aired, insults were flung, and some nasty home truths were revealed.

#7 1994–1995 MOROCCAN TOY BOY SAMIR 〔109〕

DEIRDRE MET SAMIR ON HOLIDAY IN AGADIR. HE WORKED AS A WAITER in the hotel where she stayed. It was more than a holiday fling and Samir left the sunshine of Morocco to live in Weatherfield with Deirdre. Despite the age gap and all her friends disapproving of their relationship, Deirdre and Samir wed.

When Tracy needed a kidney transplant Samir was found to be a match. On his way to hospital for the operation Samir was attacked as he walked along the canal towpath and ended up unconscious in hospital. Deirdre had to make the heartbreaking decision to turn off his life-support machine and gave her permission for his kidney to be used to save Tracy's life.

#8 2001 DEIRDRE AND DEV 〔132〕

WHEN DEIRDRE FELL for her shopkeeper boss Dev, she managed to make a complete fool of herself. After a row with Ken one night, she ended up in Dev's bed. It was an experience she wanted to repeat but Dev didn't want anything to do with her, much to Deirdre's embarrassment.

#9 1987–1991 COUNCILLOR BARLOW 〔76〕

DEIRDRE WON THE ELECTION WHEN SHE STOOD AGAINST ALF ROBERTS as an Independent candidate on Weatherfield Council. She thought Ken was supportive of her but he was only using her to split the vote so that Labour would win. Ken wasn't happy with his wife as a career woman councillor, and as Deirdre soared to dizzy heights working on the council, Ken took refuge in the arms of a woman who would become Deirdre's biggest foe: Wendy 'flaming' Crozier …

#10 1989/ 2012 WENDY CROZIER 〔80〕〔190〕

KEN'S AFFAIR WITH WENDY CROZIER WOULD BLOW HIS MARRIAGE TO Deirdre apart. In a highly tense and emotional showdown, Deirdre challenged Ken and told him she knew he was up to no good with another woman. Framed by her perm and her glasses, Deirdre's face was fierce and furious as she looked down on him, sitting in his chair. '**I want to know where you've been and who with!**' The storyline topped the Christmas TV ratings in 1989.

In 2012 Wendy returned to cause more angst for Deirdre. This time Wendy was a widow by the name of Mrs Papadopoulos, and she was after Ken once more. Word for word, in a repeat of Wendy's earlier appearance in their lives, Deirdre spat at Ken: '**I want to know where you've been, and who with!**'

The earliest photo
of Anne Kirkbride as
Deirdre Hunt, 1973

Deirdre's
LIFE ON THE STREET

1972

First appearance

DEIRDRE HUNT FIRST APPEARED ON *CORONATION STREET* IN NOVEMBER 1972. She was a vivacious, miniskirted eighteen-year-old, enjoying a drink in a pub with Jimmy Frazer. Jimmy was a business partner of Alan Howard's.

In that first scene, Deirdre's first line, uttered in what would become her trademark friendly and confident style, was: '**I think it's about time somebody bought me another drink.**'

'**That's what I like about her – dead subtle, you know. You have to watch her, you know,**' laughed Jimmy to Alan.

'**Oh, you can watch me any time you like,**' replied Deirdre. '**I've always had a fatal weakness for men with curly hair.**'

Deirdre's first scene with Jimmy and Alan placed her with two fellas who had a bit of mileage in them, age-wise. It would set a pattern for Deirdre's lifetime of romances with men much older than herself.

Deirdre only appeared in one episode of *Coronation Street* in 1972. Forty-two years later, she was still starring in and at the heart of the nation's best-loved television show.

THE REAL WORLD THIS YEAR

Edward Heath's Conservative government in power

Munich Olympics terror

Bloody Sunday in Northern Ireland

BEHIND THE SCENES

Anne Kirkbride remembered first joining *Coronation Street*. She said: 'I was down for an audition for something. And while I was there they said "Before you go, would you just nip down the corridor over to the *Coronation Street* office, they've got three lines, that's all it is, and they just need someone with a good Northern accent." They said: "If we like you we might even write you some more in, you never know."

'That was my first *Street* scene and I was petrified at the thought of coming into something I'd been watching since the age of seven.

'My very first scene was in a pub called The Vine with Alan Howard. I was the dolly bird and he was chatting to me and the sole purpose of my being there was to annoy Elsie. Then I had a brief visit to the actual street when Elsie was away and Billy Walker organised a party at No.11 as Deirdre was one of the girls invited. Then she falls asleep on the bed and Elsie comes back the next day to find this girl coming down the stairs and gets the wrong idea.'

Deirdre in her
first job at
Fairclough
& Langton's
builder's yard

1973

First job at the builder's yard

DEIRDRE'S ARRIVAL ON *CORONATION STREET* CAUSED A STIR WITH some of the Weatherfield men. She was young, confident, attractive – and nobody's fool when it came to matters of the heart.

Alan Howard flirted with Deirdre, and Alan's wife Elsie was shocked to find Deirdre asleep in her lodger Lucille Hewitt's bed! It was the morning after a party that Billy Walker arranged. At the party, Deirdre got tipsy and rested her head on Alan's shoulder when she sat next to him on the sofa.

'**Do you know what I want most in all the world?**' she asked Alan.

'**No,**' he replied.

'**Go on, ask me. Say, "What do you want most in all the world?"**'

Alan humoured her. '**What do you want most in all the world?**'

'**A wardrobe!**'

When news reached Alan's wife Elsie that her husband had been seen in the company of a young, blonde dolly bird, Elsie soon saw Deirdre off.

Alan was as shocked as Elsie to find out that Deirdre had spent the night in the house. But Elsie was livid and Deirdre had some explaining to do when Elsie caught up with her later.

GLASSES of '73

THE REAL WORLD
IN 1973
....
Britain joins the EEC
....
Princess Anne and
Mark Phillips marry
....
Tubular Bells
released
....

In the Rovers Return, Elsie leaned in conspiratorially and whispered to Deirdre: **'This is the young lady who spends the night in our house while I'm away. Have you done any more of that lately, love?'**

Deirdre replied, all polite-like: **'No, not a lot, Mrs Howard, it gets a bit boring. It's the ones who don't sleep you have to be afraid of.'**

Elsie told her: **'I've heard about sixteen different versions about what happened that night. Now I'd like the truth. What were you doing in our house? And how did you manage to get into that bed?'**

Deirdre replied: **'Oh, there were nowt clever about it. Any fool could have done it.'**

Deirdre soon caught the eye of Ray Langton and the two of them got friendly. He was planning to buy Biddulph's newsagent, which was up for sale. Ray lined Deirdre up to work there, offering her the job of shop manageress and a home in the flat above the shop too. Deirdre had been over the moon with Ray's offer: **'Eh, that's great. How can I show my undying gratitude?'**

Ray's eyes lit up. **'Well, I'm open to ideas …'** he smirked.

'Do you want any electric plugs fitting? I'm very good at that.'

It wasn't exactly what Ray had in mind.

However, Ray was outbid in his plan to buy the newsagent. The shop was bought by Len Fairclough for £3,000 and Len gave the manageress job to Rita Littlewood. He also gave her the flat above the shop and would eventually change the name from Biddulph's to the Kabin. Rita hadn't known that Ray had plans of his own for the shop, if he'd been able to buy it. She felt bad when she found out that Deirdre's offer of work there had been snatched from under her nose. Rita offered to take Deirdre on as her assistant but Ray wouldn't have it.

Rita takes on Mavis
as her assistant
in the newsagent's

Ray steeled himself to let Deirdre down gently. He had to confess that he couldn't make good on his offer of a job and a home for her after all.

Over a drink in the Rovers, Ray gave Deirdre the bad news, telling her with a shrug: **'It was Len. It was his money – he put his bird in.'**

Deirdre took the disappointing news better than Ray had expected. This elevated her in his estimation, as he had been expecting a scene.

She said: **'It's the number one rule of my life. If a fella tells you something's going to happen, don't believe it, even after it's happened. So cheer up, drink up and I'll buy you another.'**

Ray was impressed with how upbeat Deirdre was and said admiringly: **'Hey, you're a great girl.'**

She smiled back at him with: **'What took you so long?'**

After letting Deirdre down over the job and the flat, Ray felt obliged to offer Deirdre some work. She became secretary at Len Fairclough and Ray Langton's builder's yard. Deirdre proved her worth by bringing order to the chaos of their business, making it more efficient and helping it recover from the brink of bankruptcy. Fairclough & Langton were on the skids when Deirdre arrived to work there, but with her no-nonsense attitude she helped turn the business around. Her hard work, coupled

Deirdre's mum Blanche Hunt was originally played by actress Patricia Cutts

with the ability to put the kettle on at just the right time, made her very popular.

Jerry Booth worked there too and Deirdre became friendly with him. She kept referring to Jerry as the boss, but Jerry repeatedly told her he was a hired hand, just like her, that he wasn't her gaffer. Deirdre boosted his confidence, reminding Jerry that he'd sunk his savings into the builder's yard and had *every* right to call himself the boss.

Deirdre's friendship with Jerry didn't go unnoticed by Mavis Riley, who had a bit of a soft spot for Jerry. Mavis was jealous of Jerry spending so much time at work with Deirdre. She felt that her nose had been pushed right out of joint.

Mavis moaned about the situation to Rita in the Kabin. **'It's just her and him and she's got this easy way of saying things, not all wittering on and clumsy like me,'** she said, wittering on, all clumsy. **'I know he thinks she does her hair lovely 'cos he remarked on it once – and my hair won't go like that, it's been curly since I've been in the pram. The two of them, day after day in the yard, sharing cups of tea and their dinners …'**

Rita stopped Mavis in her tracks: **'Deirdre's not his type. So what if she lets him nibble on her barm cake? She's not his type, you take my word for it.'**

Deirdre chatting with
Billy in the Rovers

1974

Billy Walker – engagement

RITA WAS RIGHT: DEIRDRE AND JERRY WOULDN'T GET TOGETHER AND Mavis had nothing to worry about on that score. Deirdre wasn't interested in Jerry at all. She soon had both Ray Langton and Billy Walker, the son of Rovers landlady Annie Walker, fighting for her attention.

In the Rovers, Deirdre was playing a game of darts with Ray and Billy when the two men started flirting with her, both vying for her attention. Ray reminded Billy that

GLASSES of '74

Although Deirdre helped out Billy behind the bar briefly in 1974, she has never officially worked as a barmaid in the Rovers

he was the one paying Deirdre's wages at the builder's yard, which he assumed gave him some kind of ownership of Deirdre, but she soon put him straight: **'Hey, it's not rent-a-bird, you know!'**

As the darts game continued, Cupid's arrow landed for Deirdre when she became drawn to Billy Walker. He was older than Ray, more mature, and almost twenty years older than Deirdre. She'd fallen for an older man once again – but a little spark would always remain between her and Ray.

First kiss

OUT ON A DATE, BILLY TREATED DEIRDRE TO SIX PENN'ORTH OF CHIPS. On the drive home, Billy gave Deirdre some fashion advice that she would never heed: **'You want to trade them glasses in for some decent ones!'**

When they returned home, talk turned to romance and Billy asked her: **'How'd you like to be courted?'**

'By you?' Deirdre replied. **'Well, isn't that funny?'** and then Billy leaned in for a kiss – Deirdre's first on-screen kiss.

Ray was jealous when Deirdre got together with Billy. He asked her what made Billy so special and pointed out to her: **'You're taller than him anyway.'**

Deirdre joked: **'Well, it makes no odds when you're lying in the long summer grass with his hot breath fanning your cheek.'**

Ray wasn't convinced and said sullenly: **'What's he got that I haven't got?'**

Deirdre pointed at the garage. **'Well, he's got that garage for a start. He's not doing so bad by the look of things.'**

Ray's jealousy turned nasty and bitter. He took out his revenge over losing out on dating Deirdre by being unpleasant to her at work and when he saw her in the pub. He

Actress Maggie Jones took over the role as Deirdre's mum Blanche

even stopped her from taking time off at the builder's yard when he found out she was planning a holiday with Billy.

Deirdre was upset and angry over Ray's behaviour and one morning she told her mum Blanche she wasn't going in to work.

'It's him again, isn't it? Little Hitler down at the yard?' said Blanche.

Deirdre told her mum that being harassed by Ray at work reminded her of being bullied by Eileen Pendlebury when she was a girl at school.

She added: 'But Ray Langton isn't Eileen Pendlebury.'

'No,' Blanche said. 'He's just a bigger girl, that's all.'

Blanche slaps Ray

AFTER DEIRDRE TOLD HER MUM THAT RAY WAS UPSETTING HER AT work, Blanche decided to take matters into her own hands. No one was going to treat her daughter that way! Blanche stormed into the Rovers, where Ray had gone for a quiet lunchtime pint. Blanche's first encounter with Ray would be one he would never forget.

'Mr Langton?' she asked when she found him at the bar.

'The one and only,' he replied cockily, wondering who on earth this woman was.

'I'm Deirdre's mother. I've got something for you.'

'Something for me?'

And with that, Blanche slapped Ray across the face as hard as she could.

'And if you want another one, just try picking on Deirdre again!'

Deirdre and Billy happily courted, despite disapproval from Billy's mum, Annie Walker. Billy was the apple of Annie's eye and could do no wrong as far as she was concerned. Annie thought Deirdre was nowhere near good enough for her son. And in typical

THE REAL WORLD
IN 1974

First McDonald's
opens in London

Lord Lucan
disappears

Harold Wilson's
Labour government
wins the election

Annie style, she wasn't shy about sharing her thoughts on the matter.

But Annie was about to be brought down a peg or two when Blanche revealed that things between Deirdre and Billy might be more serious than Annie would like. Blanche called in to the Rovers to ask Annie: **'Tell me, Mrs Walker. Do you like big hats?'**

'Big hats?' Annie replied, wondering what Blanche was going on about.

'Well, we wouldn't want to clash, would we?' Blanche said. **'At the wedding.'**

Annie pursed her lips and looked pained.

Billy proposes to Deirdre

IT WAS NOT THE MOST ROMANTIC OF PROPOSALS WHEN BILLY POPPED the question. Deirdre was sitting at her typist's desk in the builder's yard when Billy called round to see her at work. Annie had spoken to Billy about the shock she'd received from Blanche, and he called to see Deirdre to tell her he'd been ticked off by his mum. But now that marriage had been mentioned, Billy asked Deirdre what she thought of the idea after all.

'Is this a proposal, Billy Walker?' she asked.

'Yeah, why not?' he replied.

'Well, it's a bit unconventional – but the answer's yes!' When their engagement was announced, Annie Walker, the grande dame of the Rovers, was not happy with the news, and cried: **'But she's just a secretary at a backstreet plumber's!'**

Billy said to his mum: **'I'm waiting for you to say "Congratulations, Billy, you've found yourself a really nice girl at last."'**

But Annie saw Deirdre as a harlot, a scarlet woman, and replied: **'They all grow up like their mothers, dear, and Blanche Hunt puts me in mind of no one so much as Elsie Tanner.'**

With the wedding date set for the following year, Deirdre planned to move in with Billy and Annie at the Rovers once they were wed. However, it didn't take long for Deirdre to become disillusioned with Billy.

The doubts started to creep in when Blanche and Annie argued over their wedding outfits. Both had bought the same colour outfit and neither of them was willing to step down and take their outfit back to the shop. Deirdre stood firm in the argument between Annie and Blanche and told Annie that the colour clash wouldn't bother her: **'The only thing concerning me right now is whether I leave my glasses on under my veil,'** said Deirdre. **'Chances are I'll be leaving them off so I'll be as blind as a bat and if I do manage to catch a glimpse of you, you'll just be a vague greenish blur.'**

Annie made a huge fuss of her colour clash with Blanche but Deirdre insisted that it didn't matter to her. **'I've never gone along with all this stuff about a girl's wedding day being the most important day in her life. I mean, the actual wedding day is just a load of rubbish, in't it? It's all tears and phoney sentiment and people you've never seen from one year's end to the next getting drunk at your expense, not to mention all the bitching that goes on behind the scenes.'**

The clash of Annie's and Blanche's wedding outfits rumbled on, and Annie moaned to Billy about what had happened. Billy told Deirdre she should ask Blanche to take

Annie and Billy
Walker

her wedding outfit back. Deirdre refused, calling Annie 'Lady Muck' and saying Annie should be the one to return her outfit. Billy and Deirdre argued over this, discovering a lot about each other that they didn't know before. Both of them stuck to their guns in a fierce display of family loyalty to their mums.

In despair, Deirdre told Billy: **'Well, well, well. Life's full of little surprises, isn't it? It's amazing all the things you can find out about a fella when you're in spitting distance of getting married to him.'**

E L S E W H E R E   I N   1 9 7 4

Majorca

Deirdre was the youngest of a group of the Street's women who went on holiday to Majorca. Rita, Mavis, Emily, Bet, Betty, Annie, Hilda and Deirdre enjoyed a holiday in the sun together after Bet won on 'Spot the Ball'. Even Deirdre's sunglasses had huge frames.

Sun, sand,
sea and specs!

Fun in the sun
in Majorca

Am-dram

Deirdre starred as Gwendolen Fairfax in the Rovers Amateur Dramatic Association's production of *The Importance of Being Earnest*. The role of Gwendolen suited Deirdre well, with the character being smart, persistent and in pursuit of goals in which she took the initiative, much like Deirdre herself. The role of Lady Bracknell was that of a powerful, arrogant, ruthless, conservative, proper older woman – which Annie Walker played to perfection. The show was produced by Emily Bishop, and Ray Langton arranged the lighting. It was a sell-out production with tickets selling like hot cakes at 30p each.

Specs appeal

When Deirdre attended Maggie Clegg and Ron Cooke's wedding, the photographer caught her eye. He chatted her up and asked her to go outside with him to have her photograph taken. Billy Walker and Ray Langton spotted what was going on and Billy turned to Ray: **'Hey, do you reckon that fella's intentions are all that honourable towards our Deirdre?'**

Ray replied: **'I reckon he'd drop dead if she took her specs off to him!'**

STREET SCENE

Maggie and Ron's wedding

1975

Break-up with Billy

WITH BILLY AND DEIRDRE'S WEDDING DATE SET FOR 1 JUNE, THINGS went from bad to worse for the warring couple. Deirdre had long been wary that if she married Billy she would be trapped in the Rovers with Annie. Finally the wedding was called off, much to Annie's relief. Billy left Weatherfield to run a wine bar in Jersey. It was the first of what would be many failed romances for Deirdre.

Making a clean break of it after splitting up with Billy, Deirdre left her job too. She stormed into the builder's yard office and typed up her letter of resignation in front of Len, Ray and Jerry. Then she threw files and papers all over the office, emptied the contents of her desk onto the floor, picked up her typewriter and chucked it down in front of the three stunned men.

'I'm fed up here! I hate this dump. I hate the job. And I hate all of yer!'

If Fairclough & Langton thought they could survive without Deirdre, then they needed to think again.

Annie Walker and her blue-eyed boy Billy

Late-night drinks with an oil-rigger

GLASSES of '75

WITH BILLY GONE, DEIRDRE WAS FOOTLOOSE AND FANCY-FREE AND made the most of being single. She met Maurice Gordon, who worked on the oil rigs. Blanche was horrified to find out that Deirdre had spent time drinking with him in his hotel room.

Blanche slaps Deirdre for staying out all night

DEIRDRE THOUGHT HER MUM'S ATTITUDE WAS OLD-FASHIONED, SAY-ing: 'Honestly, you can't half be smug when you want to. Who elevated you to holy sainted all of a sudden? Since when did you become a nun?'

'Yes, I've had blokes,' Blanche replied. 'I've never hid it from you and I've never been ashamed of it, but there's always been summat to it.'

'Oh, come on, Mother, who are you trying to kid?' asked Deirdre. 'Some of them were a right load of rubbish.'

'How would you know?' asked Blanche.

'I were only a kid but I had eyes. And if there were one or two wives lurking around in the background, that never worried you too much either.'

'We're talking about you,' Blanche reminded her.

'And you, Mother. And where all of a sudden you get the right to lecture me.'

Blanche said: 'I may have been wild and I may have been stupid but I never let myself get picked off the streets by any Tom, Dick or Harry. I never let myself get taken back to sordid hotel bedrooms by complete strangers. I never behaved like a dirty little tramp.'

'We've only got your word for that, haven't we?' said Deirdre.

And at that, Blanche slapped Deirdre hard across the face.

Despite Blanche's disapproval, it wasn't the end of Maurice Gordon in Deirdre's life. He started pestering Deirdre and it was Ray Langton who came to Deirdre's aid to fight him off.

BEHIND THE SCENES

When Ken Farrington (Billy Walker) announced he was leaving *Coronation Street*, scripts had to be quickly rewritten. When Billy left, Deirdre started dating Ray on the rebound and ended up marrying Ray instead of Billy, as had been planned.

Anne Kirkbride on Deirdre and Ray: 'There had been a sort of bond between Ray and Deirdre the whole time. There'd been this sort of little undercurrent going on which obviously speeded up considerably when they decided to marry them off. Suddenly they were in each other's arms. This vague sexual current turned into undying love. There were no hearts and flowers involved and it was all very much matter-of-fact really. But it worked.'

Engagement to Ray

DEIRDRE AND RAY STARTED DATING AND JUST A WEEK LATER, SHE shocked Blanche again: 'Guess what, Mam? I'm going to get married! It's Ray Langton. I'm going to marry Ray Langton.'

It was news that Blanche didn't take very well. She was only too aware of the problems Deirdre had encountered with Ray in the past. She couldn't understand how Deirdre could have changed her mind about Ray and agree to marry him so soon.

Blanche wasn't backward in coming forward to Deirdre about her thoughts on Ray: 'He's just a pint-and-baccy merchant, for all his airs and fancy talk. I bet he watches telly in his stocking feet, picking his nose at the same time. He's a lout

Blanche giving Deirdre some advice – but would she ever listen?

and a big mouth and a troublemaker, he's dead rough, and I bet he sleeps with his window shut. He'll not help you around the house and I wouldn't trust him with a nun!'

'Trust me, Mam, I know what I'm doing,' Deirdre replied. 'Perhaps it'll be smooth sailing from now on.'

'You'll not change him, Deirdre, if that's what you're thinking,' Blanche warned.

On the morning of her wedding to Ray, Blanche again questioned Deirdre's judgement. Deirdre replied: 'Getting married to Billy, it was like he was leading me up a path, to a house to spend the rest of my life in – with the door shut. I would just have been living there. And there's a difference between living and feeling alive.'

Blanche said: 'And where's Ray leading you?'

'Nowhere,' Deirdre replied. 'And that's what's good about it.'

Wedding to Ray

NOT FOR THE FIRST TIME, OR THE LAST TIME, DEIRDRE IGNORED Blanche's advice. She married Ray at Weatherfield Register Office on 7 July 1975. Deirdre wore an old beige skirt suit that Blanche had had to clean curry stains off earlier that day, and Blanche wore a stern expression. Len was best man and the wedding guests were Rita and Jerry. When exchanging vows, Deirdre stumbled over her words and needed help from the registrar after she faltered slightly. Ray announced in his wedding vows that he was marrying Deirdre 'to the exclusion of all others'. But it was a vow that would ring hollow and Ray's actions would ultimately end up destroying their marriage.

THE REAL WORLD
IN 1975

Margaret Thatcher becomes leader of the Conservative Party

Microsoft founded

The Sex Pistols play their first ever gig

The first episode of *Fawlty Towers* airs

The wedding reception took place in the Rovers, where Len arranged a champagne celebration party. There was a buffet spread of sausage rolls, sandwiches and a white-iced wedding cake. After the party the newly-weds missed their train and ended up spending their honeymoon with Blanche.

Deirdre punches Tricia

Tricia Hopkins
and family

IN DECEMBER 1975, TRICIA HOPKINS HAD A QUIET WORD WITH BLANCHE to tell her that she'd seen Ray flirting with another woman. The cheeky minx Tricia then started spreading rumours that Ray was having an affair with Pauline Jarvis, who was a customer at the builder's yard. Deirdre tackled Ray over Tricia's lies and he denied anything was going on. Furious, Deirdre stormed round to see Tricia, punched her in the face and gave her a black eye.

ELSEWHERE IN 1975

Dark secret?

Blanche revealed to Rita that Deirdre was chucked out of the Girl Guides. Rita asked the reason why but Blanche wasn't prepared to tell her. Unusually for Blanche, she looked embarrassed and shifty when she replied: **'Well, it's all in her past now, Rita. It's summat we don't really talk about.'**

Taking the stage

In December 1975, Deirdre starred as Dandini in the Christmas pantomime, *Cinderella*. Deirdre's mum Blanche was in charge of costumes and make-up, and music was by Ernest Bishop. The panto was produced by Rita Littlewood, who also sang all of Bet Lynch's songs while Bet mimed onstage.

How many of these pantomime cast members can you remember?

1976

First year of marriage to Ray

THE REAL WORLD IN 1976

Apple Computers launched

The Olympics take place in Montreal

Hottest UK summer since records began

First Concorde flight

The National Theatre opens

Deirdre and Ray settle into domestic bliss

Married life with Ray

Pregnancy news 1

WHEN DEIRDRE THOUGHT SHE MIGHT BE PREGNANT, THE NEWS SOON set tongues wagging amongst the local gossip-mongers. However, it was just a pregnancy scare. This didn't stop the false news about Deirdre's pregnancy spreading like wildfire around Weatherfield – but she soon put the gossips right.

Ray mused on how life could have been for him as a dad, after he'd been told by his mates about their own wives being pregnant. He told Deirdre that his mates said that pregnant women got a special glow when they were expecting, that they went all warm, soft and round. **'What, like a tub of butter?'** she said. Deirdre told Ray they'd had a lucky escape over the pregnancy scare, but the gossips didn't yet know and the rumours continued to spread that a baby was on its way.

When Deirdre went into the Kabin, Rita greeted her with: **'Hello to the lovely mother-to-be!'**

Mavis chimed in with her congratulations and told Deirdre how lucky she was, before enquiring if the pregnancy was planned or if it was a result of a night of unbridled passion with Ray.

Deirdre stopped Mavis cold: **'I take it from all that that you think I'm in the club?'**

Rita said: **'Aren't you?'**

Deirdre replied sharply: **'No!'** and walked out, leaving Mavis and Rita sighing at the counter.

In the Rovers, even Annie Walker smiled and greeted Deirdre, enquiring about her health. Ray lapped up all the free beer he'd been bought by way of congratulations, not willing yet to tell anyone the truth about the baby news.

STREET PEOPLE

Mavis in the Kabin

Rita entered the pub and she wasn't at all happy that Deirdre wouldn't tell her what Len was up to. He'd been spring cleaning, which was most unlike him. Deirdre knew full well that Len was cleaning in preparation for Elsie's return. And so, in retaliation for Deirdre keeping secrets about Len, Rita told everyone she had a surprise of her own and announced that Deirdre wasn't pregnant at all. Now everyone knew, and it was the end of free drinks for Ray – for now, anyway.

Pregnancy news 2

DEIRDRE AND RAY THREW A PARTY TO CELEBRATE DEIRDRE'S BIRTHDAY and their first wedding anniversary. At the party Deirdre gave Ray the news that she was expecting, and this time the doctor had confirmed it. Ray was over the moon with the news. He hugged Deirdre then pulled up a chair, standing on it to get everyone's attention. Ray announced to all of their party guests: **'Me and Deirdre's pregnant!'**

Maternity leave – temporary secretary

Len Fairclough

DEIRDRE'S PREGNANCY WOULD CAUSE PROBLEMS AT WORK AS Fairclough & Langton would need to hire a temporary secretary while Deirdre went on maternity leave. And if Len had any thoughts about saving a bit of money by not paying Deirdre what she was due, he would need to think again. In the builder's yard, Deirdre read Len the rules of the Employment Protection Act. She was fully clued up on what she was entitled to when she went off on maternity leave.

'You can't sack me 'cos I got pregnant. I could have you for unfair dismissal,' she said.

Ray joked to Len: **'The only idea about her having a kid was to get a tasty bit of a secretary in here.'**

To which Deirdre replied: **'Sexist pig!'**

'Is that why you took me on in the first place? 'Cos I was a tasty bit of a secretary?' she asked him later when they were in the office on their own.

'Well, I thought you were all right, as they go,' said Ray.

'Listen!' said Deirdre. **'I am the last tasty bit of a secretary ...'** She grabbed his ear and twisted it. **'The last and final one, understand?'**

'Can I have my ear back?' Ray said, grimacing. But Deirdre wasn't finished with him yet.

'And any temporary replacement for me will not be a tasty bit of a secretary. It will be a very ugly typewriting person!'

ELSEWHERE IN 1976

Ray and Deirdre clashed when Ray wanted them to move into Minnie Caldwell's old house, 5 Coronation Street. Deirdre wasn't keen on it at all. **'It's just a scruffy little house in a tatty backstreet,'** she told Ray. **'When I move I want to move up, not down.'**

'We'll get it for a song,' Ray replied.

'Well, you can sing it on your own.' she told him. However, they went to view the house together, although Deirdre kept telling Ray the house was not what she wanted, not at all. Despite Deirdre's protests, early in the following year she and Ray and their new baby moved in to No.5.

BEHIND
THE
SCENES

Anne Kirkbride and
Johnny Briggs, 1986

Filming a scene in the newsagent's with Christabel Finch as Tracy Langton, the youngest star of the show, in 1979

1977

Deirdre becomes a mum

WHEN DEIRDRE WAS RUSHED TO WEATHERFIELD GENERAL HOSPITAL with labour pains, she was alone in the ambulance. Ray was out at a dance and Deirdre couldn't reach him by phone. Much later, with Deirdre safely installed in the maternity ward, Ray barged in to see his wife. He apologised for not being there when she was brought in to hospital. Deirdre accepted his apology but told him she didn't want him in the delivery room, saying he wouldn't be of much use.

Deirdre was wheeled off to the delivery room wearing her nightie and her glasses and when they wheeled her back to her bed in her nightie with her new baby, her glasses were still firmly in place! Whether Deirdre took her specs off to give birth is a mystery that will go unsolved.

Deirdre and Ray's baby girl was born on 24 January 1977, weighing 8 pounds 4 ounces. Deirdre was over the moon with her new baby daughter, although Ray had hoped for a boy. Ray's first words to Deirdre on seeing his new daughter were: '**She looks just like your mam!**'

Blanche was Deirdre and the baby's first visitor: she was dying to take a look at her new grandchild. In a touching moment, Blanche sat on Deirdre's hospital bed and said lovingly: '**Well, what about you … with a daughter.**'

Then Deirdre replied: '**What about you … Grandma!**'

Tracy Langton's
christening

Back on the Street, Ray threw a party for friends and neighbours to celebrate the birth. Annie Walker gave a speech and then Ray addressed them all, promising them a proper party when Deirdre came out of hospital. As they all raised their glasses to celebrate the arrival of the baby, local gossip Hilda Ogden told Blanche about Deirdre being on her own when she had to call the ambulance because Ray had been out gallivanting.

There was further friction between Deirdre and Ray when it came to naming the baby. Deirdre wanted to call her Lynette but Ray chose Tracy and registered the name against Deirdre's wishes, with Lynette as her middle name. When Deirdre found out what Ray had done, she was furious. Tracy's christening was held at St Mary's and her godparents were Betty Turpin, Emily Bishop and, ironically, her future adoptive dad, Ken Barlow.

While Deirdre had been in the maternity ward, she became friendly with Sally Norton, the woman in the next bed, and they agreed they would meet up once a year on the same date. It was an agreement that would have terrifying consequences for both Deirdre and Tracy two years later.

Deirdre attacked

WHEN TRACY WAS JUST EIGHT MONTHS OLD, DEIRDRE WAS ATTACKED. As she walked home from her keep-fit class, Deirdre became aware that someone was following her and she started to run. The attacker ran after her and he collared Deirdre in a tunnel under the viaduct, where he tried to rape her. Deirdre escaped his clutches and ran home in tears. She was so shaken when she got home that she could barely speak to Ray to tell him what had happened.

The attack left Deirdre emotionally scarred and she refused to leave the house. She retreated into her own world, neglecting Tracy, ignoring Ray and refusing to go to the

Deirdre has
trouble coming
to terms with
Ray's affair

police. When Emily tried to comfort her, Deirdre brushed off her concerns, telling her that real life wasn't as nice as Emily liked to paint it.

'**Real life's perverts hanging around in back alleys,**' she told Emily. '**I know, from experience.**'

Emily suggested Deirdre might just need a rest.

'**It's not a rest I need, it's a flaming new world.**'

Deirdre saved from suicide

DEIRDRE STRUGGLED TO COPE IN THE AFTERMATH OF THE ATTACK. SHE became unbalanced and sank into a deep depression. In desperation one day, she disappeared and abandoned baby Tracy. Deirdre was found sobbing, on a bridge over a motorway, contemplating suicide. Luckily she was distracted by a passing lorry driver who asked her for directions. The interruption made Deirdre aware of the enormity of what she was about to do; she pulled herself together and went home to Ray.

She went on to have psychiatric counselling but still refused to let Ray near her. Ray blamed Deirdre for punishing him for another man's actions and their marriage would never fully recover.

E L S E W H E R E   I N   1 9 7 7

Tracy won a bonny baby competition at the community centre. Deirdre and Ray celebrated with their prize – a weekend for two in London.

Deirdre fell out with Rita over Ray's share of Fairclough & Langton. Deirdre felt the business should be split fifty-fifty but Rita insisted that Len keep his majority share of 60 per cent.

1978

Deirdre discovers Ray's affair

AS DEIRDRE'S LIFE REVOLVED AROUND BEING A WIFE AND MOTHER, she saw herself as little more than 'Ray's missus'. Her future might not have been rosy but at least it was settled and secure. However, just when it looked like Deirdre's life was stable again, her world was rocked when she found out that Ray was having an affair. It would throw her life into turmoil again.

Ray swore that his relationship with Janice Stubbs, a waitress at Dawson's cafe, was platonic, but he was lying.

It was Emily who first told Deirdre that she had seen Ray getting friendly with Janice in the cafe, enjoying a chat and a laugh. But as far as Emily was concerned, Ray and Janice were just friends. However, Deirdre was suspicious that there was something going on as Ray was spending more time outside of the house. She decided to investigate further to find out for herself. Deirdre went to Dawson's cafe and confronted Janice: '**You know who I am, don't you? Mrs Langton. Ray's wife.**'

Janice stood her ground: she didn't see the need to explain herself, and as a single woman she said that she didn't see herself at fault. She told Deirdre if she wanted to speak to anyone, she should talk to Ray.

THE REAL WORLD
IN 1978

First test-tube
baby born

First episode
of *Grange Hill*
broadcast

Host Argentina wins
the World Cup

Ray with his mistress
Janice Stubbs

Deirdre tells Ray she's leaving him

DEIRDRE DECIDED TO TACKLE RAY AND WENT OFF IN SEARCH OF HIM IN town. When she found him she gave him what for and told him to get back to his fancy piece. She knew he had been lying, and she had fallen for his lies when he told her he was working overtime or playing snooker matches. All the while he had been with Janice.

Back home, Deirdre packed her bags and told Ray she was leaving him.

'I'm packing, I'm taking Tracy and I'm leaving. You've been messing about with that girl at Dawson's. And as usual the wife is the last one to know. But I do know and I'm leaving you and it's as simple as that.'

Ray tried to interrupt but Deirdre carried on, in full flow now: 'At least do me a favour and don't lie to me like you have been doing these last few weeks. Muggins here believed it all! I was fool enough to think I had a husband I can trust.'

Deirdre gives Ray a second chance

RAY TOLD DEIRDRE HE WAS FINISHED WITH JANICE. HE EVEN SWORE ON Tracy's life that his fling was over and done with and he begged her for another chance. Deirdre relented, for Tracy's sake more than anything, and gave Ray and their marriage another go.

However, it didn't work out as Deirdre had hoped. When Ray was offered a new job in the Netherlands, Deirdre was all packed and set to leave Weatherfield with him and start again, overseas. But at their leaving party in the Rovers, Deirdre changed her mind. She broke down and announced to a shocked Ray that she wouldn't be going with him after all.

GLASSES of '78

Blanche demanded to know what was going on and asked Deirdre why she had changed her mind. 'Holland, China, it wouldn't make any difference,' Deirdre told her mum. 'Because we're finished, that's why. Him and me are finished.'

Blanche begged Deirdre to give it a try and make a fresh go of her marriage with Ray but Deirdre was firm. '**It's no good, I just can't forgive him for what he did,**' she said. '**I can never trust him again and without trust there's no point. All I can hear is a voice saying, "It's no good, you don't love him any more. It's a sham, you'd better finish it now," and that's what I'm doing.**'

Despite Blanche's pleas for Deirdre to stay with her husband, Deirdre was not prepared to compromise. But she did confide to Blanche the real reason why she was not prepared to settle and start again with Ray. In a heartfelt speech to her mother she summed up all her feelings about the attack and about Ray's affair …

'I was happy, blissfully happy. We were like Starsky and Hutch, a team. We used to eat off the same plate, I used to finish his sentences for him, his thoughts even. We had it that much together. The world outside was something you just had to waste your time on now and again to earn a living or buy food. The real world was here – him, me and Tracy. It was perfect. My whole body were laughing from morning to night. And then there were that fella ... the real world stuck its fist through one of my windows. But I got over it. It wasn't easy, I felt different but I got over it. And then there was her. Janice. I just couldn't believe it. I mean, call me naive if you like, I know anything goes these days but I couldn't understand how he could possibly be unfaithful to me. It was like that fella all over again. My whole body was freezing, my heart was dead – and I won't get over it this time, because I could understand that fella in a way but I'll never understand Ray. He had me and he went to her. I loved Ray too much. How could he be like all the rest? How could he?'

Ray leaves for the Netherlands

RAY LEFT FOR THE NETHERLANDS ON HIS OWN and he left without even saying goodbye to Tracy. '**Tell her I'll see her when I can,**' he told Deirdre as he headed out the door. Deirdre and Tracy would not see Ray again until 2005, when he returned to the Street with shock news.

With Ray gone, Deirdre was financially broke and could no longer afford to live at No.5 on her own. She and Tracy moved in with Emily at No.3 and Deirdre would become one of the first single mums in British soap.

But she wouldn't be single for long.

BEHIND THE **SCENES**

Almost the end of Deirdre

When Neville Buswell (Ray Langton) announced he was leaving *Coronation Street* it was almost the end of Deirdre too. Bill Podmore, the *Coronation Street* producer at the time, told Anne Kirkbride that after six years in the show Deirdre would be written out. The idea was that Tracy and Deirdre would leave the show with Ray as the Langton family started a new life in the Netherlands. However, Neville Buswell persuaded *Coronation Street* to keep Deirdre in the show.

Anne Kirkbride: 'The producer knocked on my door and said, "You know Neville's leaving, and you're going to have to go as well I'm afraid. We can't find a way to keep you."

'They didn't know what they were going to do with me, because they'd already got a lot of single women on the *Street*. And that was the end of it.'

Deirdre
about **Ken**:
'Me and Ken, it's like we were always meant to walk beside one another.'

Deirdre *to* **Ken**
when they make up after one of their many fights:

'Even though you get on my nerves and we argue like cat and dog, it's still you I want, when the chips are down.'

Ken:
'I want us to grow
old together.'
Deirdre:
'We *are* old.'
Ken:
'I want us to grow
really old together.'

Deirdre *to* **Ken**:
'Does it make
you feel a
bit more BA
Honours
wearing your
brogues?'

Deirdre *to* **Ken**:
'God, Ken, is it really a
whole year since Amy
was born? I tell you, I've
aged ten years this year.
I look in the mirror and
I just see my mother
staring back at me.'

Deirdre:
'I like Kirk
Douglas. I like
his chin.'
Ken:
'Chins are
over-rated.'

Deirdre *to* **Ken**
*talking about her work as PA
in the council:*

'I've had Julie
and Donna
fighting over a
mouse mat and
using me as a
go-between.'

Deirdre
to **Ken**
on their second wedding day:

'I love you
more than
any man
I've ever
known.'

Somehow Ken rarely managed to say the right thing

Ken *to* **Deirdre**:

'You can't resist them, can you, Deirdre? You seem to pick the most unreliable boyfriends. It's your choice of slimy bed partners that gets you into trouble!'

Deirdre *to* **Eileen** *about* **Ken**:

'I've got very good legs. Ken likes my legs. In fact, he likes everything about me. He's lovely. I do love him.'

Deirdre *to* **Ken** *when she found out that transsexual Hayley and Roy could be wed legally due to a change in the law:*

'Do they sell a card in the Kabin for that?'

Deirdre:
'I've got a couple of marrows, some mince and some couscous.'
Ken: 'So?'
Deirdre:
'So I'm doing stuffed marrow.'
Ken:
'Do you think that's wise?'

Team work

Deirdre *and* **Ken** *argued when he offered to bring her a library book:*

'I don't have time to read.'

'You've got plenty of time to smoke!'

1979

Lorry crashes into the Rovers

DEIRDRE WAS CENTRE STAGE IN ONE OF *CORONATION STREET*'S MOST explosive storylines in 1979. The lorry crash at the Rovers was one of the soap's major storylines that year. Many characters were injured and Alf Roberts was knocked unconscious and in a coma for weeks. For the Langtons, the lorry crash would involve little Tracy in her first major storyline and would see Deirdre brought to the brink of desperation once more.

In March 1979, Deirdre put two-year-old Tracy in her pushchair and walked down the Street to the Rovers. Deirdre was with Sally Norton, the woman she'd been in the next bed to in the maternity ward when she had given birth to Tracy. All that Deirdre had planned to do was pop into the pub to talk to Annie Walker about a knitting pattern. It was an outing that should have taken no more than a few minutes, but it ended up throwing Deirdre's life into danger and chaos. Saying goodbye to Sally, Deirdre left Tracy in her pushchair outside the pub, as Annie didn't allow children in the bar. She went through to see Annie in the back room and had only been there a few minutes when the pub was rocked by what felt like an explosion.

There was an almighty screech followed by a loud thud and the smashing of glass. **'What on earth ... ?'** Annie muttered, dazed with shock.

A lorry driver had suffered a heart attack and died at the wheel as he was driving along Coronation Street. The lorry careered off the road and overturned on the cobbles outside the pub, and its load of timber crashed through the front windows of the Rovers.

Ken helps lead Deirdre
away from danger

Deirdre is convinced that Tracy has been crushed by the wreckage

The residents look on as Deirdre searches for Tracy

The noise from the crash panicked everyone, and Deirdre knew straight away that she had to get to Tracy. There was smoke and dust everywhere and it was hard to see where she was going, but Deirdre forced her way through to the front of the pub, past bar staff and customers who had been thrown to the floor. Deirdre knew she had to get out of the pub. Whatever had happened, she had to find Tracy.

Deirdre pulled the pub door open. But in the spot where she'd left Tracy's push-chair there was now a pile of wood that had crashed down from the lorry. Tracy was nowhere to be seen. The lorry was on its side, its windows smashed and the driver dead. Everywhere was chaos. As the regulars inside the Rovers tried to help each other cope with what had happened, above the crying and the tears could be heard one voice louder than all the rest. It was Deirdre, screaming over and over, **'Tracy! Tracy!'** and desperately looking for her daughter.

Deirdre clawed and pulled at the fallen timber with her bare hands, in sheer panic, searching for Tracy. The police and an ambulance were soon on the scene and Deirdre was led away in tears by Emily and Ena Sharples when it became clear that Deirdre's attempts to find Tracy were futile. At Emily's house Deirdre's panic soon turned to deep shock and she sat in silence, convinced that Tracy was dead.

'I only left her for a minute,' she told Emily and Ena, when they tried to comfort her. **'It wasn't even a minute.'** Emily held Deirdre's hand as they waited for news from the police but, despite Emily's words of comfort, Deirdre remained certain that she would never see her daughter again, repeating over and over: **'She's dead, she is. Tracy's dead.'**

Deirdre cuddled Tracy's pink teddy bear close to her and started blaming herself …

'It's my fault. I started it. I split us all up, didn't I?
First there was me and Ray. I sent him away, it's all
my fault. I started it. Families should stick together.
That's what families are for. They're like flowers,
like that. Take one petal away and it's all gone.'

Ena Sharples

Ena, as was her way, was firm with Deirdre and told her: '**I still don't believe Tracy's dead.**'

Deirdre said: '**Dead. That's the word, isn't it? Family's dead, so she's dead too. It follows, it's logical. How are we going to tell Ray? He adored her.**'

But Ena would not be moved. She was determined not to let Deirdre think the worst and said: '**There's going to be nowt to tell him.**'

Tracy is kidnapped

WITH DEIRDRE UNABLE TO HOLD BACK HER TEARS, THERE WAS A knock at the door and Emily went to answer. Ken was there with a policeman who gave Emily good news. All of the wood had been moved from the front of the pub and there was no sign of Tracy ever having been there. Emily ran through to the living room to share the joy with Deirdre, crying: '**Deirdre! Tracy's alive! She's alive!**' but Deirdre had gone. She had disappeared out the back door and walked away down the ginnel, heading towards the canal.

The police found Tracy in a park with Sally Norton. Tracy was safe and well and blissfully unaware of the drama that had unfolded back on the Street. Sally had taken Tracy from outside the Rovers after Deirdre had left her there, and she had wheeled Tracy away in her pushchair. Sally was mentally unwell and had already had her own son placed into care. She had taken Tracy without permission or anyone's knowledge, but had ultimately saved her life.

Sally Norton

The police took Tracy back to Emily's, where Ena Sharples was doing her best to stop Emily from worrying and crying. In her typical no-nonsense style, Ena told Emily to shut up: '**Deirdre will want a calm, quiet host to come back to, not the Wailing Wall of Weatherfield!**'

Deirdre saved from suicide (again)

THE POLICE THEN FOUND DEIRDRE ON A CANAL TOWPATH UNDER A bridge. As Deirdre edged towards the water, a policewoman quietly approached along the towpath. '**Mrs Langton?**' she said. '**We've got the baby.**'

Deirdre did not move: she was still in despair, still contemplating ending her life by walking into the murky depths of the canal. The policewoman tried again: '**We've got Tracy,**' but still Deirdre did not respond.

Emily arrived with Len and when it became clear that Deirdre still did not believe the news that Tracy was alive, Len raced back to the Street in his van and returned with Tracy.

It was only when Deirdre heard Tracy cry that she turned to see her daughter and rushed to her, holding her in her arms and crying with relief.

BEHIND THE SCENES

Anne Kirkbride recalled filming the lorry crash at the Rovers: 'There was this lorry upside down with all this wood and a big hole in the front of the Rovers. The wheels were spinning on the lorry. It really got to me. You knew it wasn't a real place but in your mind somewhere it was and it was as if it was really happening. That was the effect it was supposed to have on people and just for a moment I had a little shiver.

'I spent two days shouting "Tracy!" stood on a pile of wood with smoke being pumped out. It was easy to do because the whole thing was horrifically real. It was easy to be traumatised in that situation and to actually feel you were desperately searching, that under all that wood was a little girl. I remember I lost my voice. I'd completely strained my voice and I had to rest it totally. It just came back to me in time for studio on Friday.'

Would Deirdre fall for Billy's charms again?

Billy Walker asks Deirdre to move to Jersey

Ken Barlow befriended Deirdre during the aftermath of the lorry crash and provided her with a shoulder to lean on. The depth of her feelings for Ken took Deirdre by surprise. However, any notions of romance between the two of them at this stage were put to one side when Billy Walker returned. It wasn't long before Deirdre and Billy decided to get back together. He offered to take Deirdre away from Weatherfield to live with him in Jersey.

Billy's mum, Annie, was not at all happy to hear this news as she still thought little of Deirdre. She had always thought Billy was far too good for the likes of Deirdre, who was now a single mum and therefore even further down Annie's scale of what was good enough. Emily was also disappointed when Deirdre told her she was thinking of getting back with Billy. Emily thought Ken was a much better choice for Deirdre, being older and more stable.

Annie Walker was prepared to do anything to make sure that single mum Deirdre did not get her claws into her son. And so when Billy asked his mum for a loan of £2,000 to invest in a wine bar in Jersey, she told him she would give him the money on one condition – that he returned to Jersey without Deirdre. Billy thought this was ludicrous and refused to consent to his mum's demand. That is, until Deirdre told him that she thought he wasn't as exciting as her first husband Ray had been. Billy then stormed off to Jersey on his own, with Annie's money and her blessing.

Deirdre dates Ken

WITH DEIRDRE'S PREFERENCE FOR THE OLDER MAN SHINING THROUGH again, she took a fancy to Mike Baldwin in 1979 and went out on a few dates. But it was to be another man in the shape of Ken Barlow she was eventually drawn to. The pair of them even went off to the Lake District on holiday. They also attended Gail Potter's wedding to Brian Tilsley together. They sat in the church at Gail's wedding,

STREET SCENE

Gail Potter marries Brian Tilsley, the first in a *very* long line husbands!

Deirdre enjoys a drink
in the Rovers with Ken

Deirdre with one failed marriage behind her and Ken, a widower following the deaths of wives Valerie and Janet.

    '**You look very solemn, Ken,**' Deirdre told him.

    '**Well, it's a solemn occasion,**' he replied.

    '**As we both know,**' she said.

    Ken would always have a rival for Deirdre's affections in the form of Mike, the local lothario and *Coronation Street* Casanova. Over time the rivalry between Ken and ladies' man Mike would develop into something much more intense.

Gossiping with Gail
in the café

HAPPY FAMILIES

THERE WERE PLENTY OF HAPPY TIMES for Deirdre in the Barlow household, despite all the trouble and strife. Whether it was her errant daughter, wayward husband or battleaxe mother, Deirdre had a lot to put up with. But it wasn't all bad and there are many memories of the good times in Deirdre's family life.

Deirdre and Tracy

Ken adopted Deirdre's daughter Tracy

Deirdre inherited frumpy Albert Tatlock when she married Ken

Tracy welcomed back into the family by Deirdre and Ken

Ken's 60th birthday, 1999

Amy Barlow's 1st birthday party, 2005

Merry Christmas from the Barlow household, 2005

Deirdre working
behind the counter
with Alf in the
corner shop

1980

Working at the corner shop

DEIRDRE STARTED WORK AT THE CORNER SHOP, ALF'S MINI-MARKET. She sometimes took Tracy into work with her, where Tracy would sit on the shop counter with her colouring book. Shopkeeper Alf Roberts was very happy with his new assistant and commented to Ken that Deirdre had even managed to shift some of the jars of red cabbage he'd had on the shelf for years. Ken looked embarrassed when he heard this as Deirdre had already used her charms to sell him one of the jars.

Working in the shop ensured Deirdre found out all the local gossip and she often served up wisdom and advice along with the groceries. Deirdre had her first row in the shop when Elsie stormed in to complain that Deirdre had sold cider to her grandson, Martin Cheveski, who was only sixteen years old. Deirdre replied that Martin had said the cider was for Elsie, but Elsie denied it. She blasted Deirdre for selling booze to underage kids.

'**He was in here just the other week for a bottle of gin!**' Deirdre told Elsie. '**That was for you, I hope?**'

Elsie hung her head and said quietly, '**Yes, that was for me.**'

Alf defended Deirdre against Elsie's tirade and she finally apologised to Deirdre. After Elsie left the shop Alf asked Deirdre: '**Is that the first bit of aggro you've had in here?**'

Deirdre nodded yes.

'**It gets worse than that, believe me,**' he said.

GLASSES of '80

Ken and Deirdre date

AS A WORKING SINGLE MUM, DEIRDRE BECAME THE CENTRE OF ATTEN-tion for eligible bachelors in the Street, Ken more so than anyone. Deirdre and Ken became close and she hinted strongly to him that if he were to propose, she would accept. However, this had the opposite effect than Deirdre had expected. It scared Ken off, as he thought he was too old for her and he didn't want to risk a third marriage at his age. His first wife, Valerie, had died after being electrocuted, and his second wife Janet committed suicide.

Deirdre the entrepreneur

IN AN EFFORT TO MAKE SOME MONEY TO SUPPORT HERSELF AND HER baby, gutsy single mum Deirdre turned entrepreneur. She set up the Coronation Street Secretarial Bureau along with Emily Bishop, and the two of them carried out typing and accountancy services for local businesses. One of their first customers was Jeff 'Fangio' Bateman, who took Deirdre out on a date.

ELSEWHERE IN 1980

Working woman

Deirdre worked temporarily in the Kabin, helping Mavis out while Rita was away. She was Mavis's assistant, sharing cups of tea behind the counter and supporting Mavis when she received obscene phone calls from a stranger.

Deirdre also worked, very briefly, at Weatherfield Rainwear. She had to quit almost as soon as she'd started as Emily didn't feel able to look after Tracy full-time.

Emily gets wed

When Emily wed Arnold Swain at Weatherfield Register Office, Deirdre stood at Emily's side as her witness.

Babysitting blues

Deirdre dated Alan Skidmore, who worked as Mike Baldwin's sales manager in London. Alan chatted up Deirdre as she struggled with Tracy's pushchair one day. He said if she refused his offer of help he would be thrown out of the RSPBB – the Royal Society for the Protection of Beautiful Birds. Despite his corny chat-up lines, Deirdre agreed to go out with him. Alan was soon put off when Deirdre couldn't get a babysitter and brought Tracy along on their date.

1981

Deirdre and Dirk the Dutchman

DIRK VAN DER STEK, A COLLEAGUE OF RAY'S FROM THE NETHERLANDS, came over to the UK on business. Deirdre met up with him and she and Dirk ended up having a fling. Ken was livid: he was insanely jealous about Dirk and Deirdre's relationship.

STREET PEOPLE

Emily and Arnold

Deirdre dates Mike

Deirdre drops Ken for Mike

ONE NIGHT, DEIRDRE WAS ALL DOLLED UP AND WAITING IN THE ROVERS for Ken to arrive to take her out on a date. She waited ... and she waited but there was no sign of Ken, not even a phone call to explain where he was. Mike came into the pub, found out that Deirdre had been stood up and offered to take her out himself. **'The Jag's outside – why not join me?'** he offered.

And she did, telling the regulars: **'If Ken comes in, tell him I couldn't wait.'**

When Ken finally reached the pub, he explained that his car had broken down on the Moors and he couldn't reach a phone. He was furious to hear Deirdre had gone out with Mike.

Ken tried asking Deirdre out again when his car was fixed, but she was very cool towards him. **'I'm sorry, Ken, I can't, I've got plans. I don't just sit in every night waiting for you to take me out.'** Her plans were a night with Mike, who called round to see her with a bottle of wine. Emily wasn't happy that Deirdre was going out with Mike – she had always thought Ken was a much wiser choice. But when Emily voiced her concerns to Deirdre, all she heard in reply was: **'At least with a wolf in wolf's clothing, a girl knows where she is.'**

Ken had a quiet word in the pub with Mike about his intentions towards Deirdre. He wanted to know if Mike was serious about her or whether he was just stringing her along. **'The situation is that I've taken her out a few times,'** Mike said. **'It's worked, we've had a ball. I've been quite surprised how much of a ball we've had.'**

Ken gave Mike a stern look, left his untouched beer on the counter and walked out in a jealous rage.

Deirdre turns down Ken's proposal

KEN KNEW THAT HE HAD TO SPEAK TO DEIRDRE, TO FIND OUT WHAT was really going on. He had to know if she was developing feelings for Mike or whether there was any chance for himself.

At first, Deirdre told Ken she liked being a free agent and Ken revealed how upset he was to hear her say this. **'I'm wildly jealous!'** he cried. **'I'm jealous to the pit of my stomach. I need to think of you with affection, love, and certainly not with frustration, anger and uncertainty. I can't bear that, Deirdre, I can't.'**

Deirdre told him: **'Look, Ken. I've got a life going for me that's pleasant. I'm not prepared to—'**

But Ken cut her short with a shock proposal. **'Not even if we got engaged?'**

'Engaged?' Deirdre replied, stunned. **'That's something else altogether!'**

However, Deirdre turned Ken's proposal down, telling him he was too unreliable. But Ken was not about to give up on her just yet.

Deirdre realises Ken is the man for her

AFTER HAVING HIS PROPOSAL TURNED DOWN BY DEIRDRE, KEN STARTED going out with beautician Sonia Price. Deirdre continued casually seeing Mike and helped him move in to his new flat. At Mike's flat-warming party, Ken and Sonia turned up together but Mike took a fancy to Sonia and she left Ken to be with Mike. As Mike flirted with Ken's date, Deirdre and Ken were left on their own. They ended up in Mike's kitchen, doing the washing-up together and enjoying each other's company.

Deirdre dumps Mike

THE MORNING AFTER THE FLAT-WARMING PARTY, MIKE POPPED IN TO Alf's Mini-Market to see Deirdre. He wanted to explain about going off with Sonia, and joked: **'I'm just a misunderstood lad in search of love.'**

Deirdre told him she wasn't going to be a sucker for his charm, not this time.

Mike sighed: **'I'm no Omar Sharif.'**

Deirdre replied: **'Dead right. And I'll tell you something. If Omar Sharif did what you did last night I'd say, "Omar kid, on your camel!"'**

Mike tried to apologise but Deirdre stood firm and told him she wasn't going to be taken for granted again. She told him she wanted to finish their relationship. **'I think we've come to the end of something, no hard feelings. It's been fun and it was nice while it lasted. But it's not going anywhere, it's not what I want, so I think we'd better just call it a day.'**

Mike accepted Deirdre's decision but before he walked out of the shop he left Deirdre with his parting shot: **'Like you said, it was nice while it lasted, it was fun. But I'll tell you something, I don't think you're going to have half as much fun in life with the Ken Barlows of this world. See you around.'**

Deirdre accepts Ken's second proposal

KEN WAS OVER THE MOON TO HEAR DEIRDRE AND MIKE HAD SPLIT UP and he took her for a drink in the Rovers to celebrate. He whisked Deirdre away on holiday to Scotland to introduce her to his late wife Valerie's family. While they were on holiday, Ken popped the question again and this time Deirdre accepted.

Deirdre marries Ken – Husband #2

KEN AND DEIRDRE BECAME ONE OF THE BEST-LOVED PARTNERSHIPS ON television. More than 15 million viewers tuned in to watch Deirdre Langton say 'I do' to Ken Barlow on 27 July 1981. They were married at All Saints church in Weatherfield, with Deirdre given away by Alf.

Before she headed to the church, Deirdre gathered her thoughts in Emily's living room when Alf called in to escort her to the wedding car. In a touching moment, he told Deirdre how lucky he thought Ken was. He said it wasn't just because Deirdre was an attractive young woman, but because she had 'put a bit of a bubble into Ken's life', just as she had done with Alf over the last few months, after his wife Renee had died in a car crash. Deirdre gave Alf a peck on the cheek and told him: **'You're not so bad as a substitute dad, you know.'**

At the wedding service, Deirdre looked radiant in a blue dress and with flowers in her hair. It was one of the rare occasions where she took her glasses off, entrusting them to Alf to look after. Len was best man, Emily was matron of honour and Deirdre's daughter Tracy and Ken's daughter Susan were bridesmaids. Ken and Deirdre were a perfect match – even Blanche approved.

Ken and Deirdre's
wedding day. Can you
name all the characters?

Cutting the cake
at their wedding
reception in
the Rovers

Ken and Deirdre's 1981 wedding took place two days before HRH Prince Charles married Lady Diana Spencer – and their *Coronation Street* wedding beat the royal wedding in the TV ratings. Deirdre noted that the age difference between her and Ken was the same as that between Charles and Diana.

Anne Kirkbride: 'When they put Deirdre together with Ken, I was thrilled, I was delighted. I'd done scenes working with him and I just thought I was so, so lucky.

'It was very special, very exciting. There was a lot of excitement in the air generally during that time because of the royal wedding and it was the middle of summer. It was a good time.'

As the vicar pronounced Deirdre and Ken husband and wife, he ended the ceremony with the words: **'Those whom God has joined together, let no man put asunder.'** It was a wedding vow that would soon be tested.

The reception was held at the Rovers, where Deirdre stood to make a speech, along with Ken's groom's speech and Len's best man speech. The guests raised their glasses to Deirdre's words as she said of her speech: **'If it goes against tradition, not to mention etiquette, well, it is 1981 and us girls have got tongues in our heads.'**

The happy couple jetted off to Corfu on honeymoon.

GLASSES of '82

1982

Friction for the newly-weds

THE BUBBLE OF DEIRDRE AND KEN'S WEDDED BLISS SOON BURST WHEN they settled down to everyday life at 1 Coronation Street. Deirdre's life revolved around working in the corner shop and then cooking and cleaning for and looking after Tracy and Ken. She also had Albert Tatlock to look after at No. 1.

Deirdre inherited Uncle Albert as an honorary family member when she married Ken. Albert wasn't even a relative of Ken's, he was the uncle of Ken's first wife Valerie who had died. But Deirdre cared for him and accepted him as part of Ken's life. In the corner shop, Alf joked to Deirdre: **'It doesn't stop, does it? First you're slaving all morning for me and then you're slaving over a hot stove for him.'** Alf meant the comment in jest but Deirdre didn't see the funny side. She had already started to feel that Ken was taking her for granted.

Uncle Albert Tatlock with Deirdre and Ken

Deirdre starts to feel Ken is taking her for granted

Deirdre defies Ken

IN HIS CAPACITY AS DEVELOPMENT OFFICER AT THE COMMUNITY Centre, Ken was asked by the police to keep a lookout for youngsters throwing their money around, as there was a team of muggers on the loose. Deirdre noticed that local lad Raymond Attwood seemed suddenly well-off when he called in to the corner shop and informed Ken, who refused to contact the police with just a flimsy suspicion.

When Betty Turpin was mugged, beaten up and had her handbag snatched in a brutal attack, she ended up in Weatherfield General Hospital, bruised and battered by her assailant. Deirdre was incensed when she found out what had happened to Betty and furious when Ken still refused to give Attwood's name to the police. Deirdre felt Ken was wrong and she defied him by going to the police herself to turn Raymond in. Ken's objections were silenced when the police confirmed that Attwood was indeed Betty's attacker.

Becoming increasingly frustrated with Ken during the first year of their marriage, Deirdre moaned to Emily that Ken wouldn't go away with her for Christmas. She wanted to go to her mum's, while Ken made them stay in Weatherfield as he wanted to go to a dance he'd arranged. Emily tried to smooth Deirdre's frustration: '**It is the season of goodwill to all men, Deirdre, even stubborn husbands.**'

Deirdre's frustration with Ken continued to grow. After just a few months of marriage, she was restless and bored with him and her married life. And that's when she looked to an old friendship for some excitement.

After Christmas, Ken had promised to take Deirdre to the pictures to see *On Golden Pond*, but he decided to stay in the house to watch a documentary on television instead. Deirdre was furious with him and went to the pictures on her own. On the way back home, she called at Mike's flat and they shared a drink together. It was one drink on one evening over one cosy chat – but it would lead to Deirdre and Ken's world being turned upside down in the months to come.

THE REAL WORLD
IN 1982

The Falklands War

Michael Jackson's *Thriller* released

Italy wins the World Cup in Spain

Sinclair ZX Spectrum goes on sale

Channel 4 launched

1983

Affair with Mike Baldwin

GLASSES of '83

WITHIN A YEAR AND A HALF OF HER MARRIAGE TO KEN, DEIRDRE HAD spent the first of what would be many cosy nights with Mike at his flat. He offered Deirdre a taste and a vision of something else, something more exciting, something more romantic, something other than Ken.

When Deirdre spent time with Mike, she lied to Ken that she was going out with a friend. Ken didn't even look up from his newspaper when Deirdre went out on her illicit dates with Mike, he was taking her for granted so much. While Ken was at home watching documentaries and doing his crosswords, Deirdre was out gallivanting with Mike. He treated her to posh meals in fancy restaurants, the kind that had linen napkins and toothpicks. This was a different world for Deirdre and she loved it.

However, it would all come to an end when the guilt overwhelmed her and she dropped a bombshell on Ken, confessing about her affair with Mike.

'**I don't want a boring life,**' Deirdre revealed to Ken. '**I don't just want to go through the motions.**'

Ken: '**What else do you want?**'

Deirdre: '**What I've found.**'

Ken: '**What's that?**'

Deirdre: '**Somebody else.**'

Ken: '**Who?**'

Deirdre: '**Mike. Mike Baldwin.**'

Deirdre's confession about Mike would blow her marriage to Ken apart

Love triangle with Ken and Mike

THE REAL WORLD
IN 1983

Shergar kidnapped

Brinks Mat robbery

The Walton
sextuplets are born

Culture Club's
'Karma Chameleon' is
the top-selling single

OVER 18 MILLION VIEWERS TUNED IN TO WATCH THE LOVE TRIANGLE of Deirdre, Ken and Mike. The storyline gripped a nation of fans and created headlines in the national press.

The *Daily Mirror* hailed it '**The most explosive, romantic situation in the history of *Coronation Street*.**'

The *Sunday Mirror* appointed a marriage guidance counsellor who advised: '**Don't be too hasty, Deirdre.**'

The *Sun* asked a computer to predict if Ken and Deirdre would stay the course. The paper even claimed that the Queen had phoned Buckingham Palace from abroad to demand that *Coronation Street* be taped and flown out to her.

The Times ran a history of Ken and Deirdre's storyline for its readers who might have missed some saucy details from the tabloids.

Poet Laureate Sir John Betjeman, a devoted *Street* fan, said: '**I think Ken is a nice man and deserves better.**'

The *Manchester Evening News* TV critic compared the story with the nineteenth-century realist playwright Henrik Ibsen and said: '**I rather think Ibsen comes off second best.**'

The *Guardian* reported that a Chesterfield theatre sold only one ticket for a play that was showing the same night as '**Ken and Deirdre were on the telly**'.

Ken was shocked and confused when Deirdre revealed her frustration with the marriage and couldn't understand why she wanted more than what he was offering her.

Deirdre explained to a stunned Ken that Mike talked to her and listened to her in a way that Ken never had. She told him that she thought he simply tolerated her now. She felt she might as well have been part of the furniture as far as Ken was concerned. As she tried to explain her feelings to Ken, the phone rang and Deirdre answered it. It was clear to Ken that his wife was talking to Mike on the phone and she quickly hung up. Ken reeled as he took in Deirdre's confession, and then his disbelief and shock turned into anger.

Ken demands to know what's going on when Deirdre takes the call from Mike

FROM SCRIPT TO SCREEN:

CORONATION STREET   EP#2284   TX:21/02/1983

KEN

Baldwin of all people! You decide to have
an affair to enliven the tedium of your
marriage and you have to go and pick a
little creep like him.

DEIRDRE

I didn't pick him! I didn't go looking for
an affair. I didn't want an affair!

KEN

Oh I see. Was it an irresistible impulse?
Was it written in the stars? Was this
thing bigger than the both of you?

DEIRDRE

I hate you when you talk like that.

KEN

What you hate is the truth! About your
sordid little bit on the side with a spiv
like Baldwin.

DEIRDRE

At least he's human. At least he wanted
me.

KEN
    (explodes)
I WANTED YOU!

DEIRDRE

You never wanted me, Ken, or kids or
anything. It's your pride that's hurt,
that's all.

KEN

That's not true, I'm afraid. I love you.

A KNOCK AT THEIR FRONT DOOR. THEY BOTH IGNORE IT.

KEN

I'm the man you married. I'm exactly the
same now as I was then and if that wasn't
what you wanted, why did you marry me?

DEIRDRE

Oh, Ken.

ANOTHER URGENT KNOCK AT THE DOOR.

KEN

Ignore it.

DEIRDRE

No.

DEIRDRE OPENS THE DOOR. MIKE IS STOOD THERE.

MIKE

Why did you put the phone down on me?

DEIRDRE

It's Ken. He knows. I told him everything.

*DEIRDRE TRIES TO CLOSE THE DOOR AGAINST MIKE BUT HE
HOLDS IT OPEN AGAINST HER AS KEN YANKS DEIRDRE BACK
INTO THE HOUSE, BACK TOWARDS HIM AND AWAY FROM MIKE.*

DEIRDRE

Ken! Please!

KEN

Shut up!

Ken slammed the door shut against Mike and in his rage, threw Deirdre up against the wall. She struggled free from Ken and ran from him, sitting and crying at the kitchen table.

Reeling from her revelation, Ken accused Deirdre of deceit and lies and struggled to understand why she wanted more from their marriage than he could give. He accused her of killing their marriage and told her to pack her bags and go.

Deirdre brought her suitcases downstairs and told Ken she was going to stay with her mum ...

KEN
You're ending our marriage, you're breaking up our family, just to go to your mother's. I mean, what does that solve?

DEIRDRE
It gets me out of here, it gets me away from you. That's what you said you wanted, for me to go.

KEN
Yes, because of what you've done. Because of what you think of our marriage. And don't you go trying to tell me that I'm the one who's ending this thing. It's your doing, it's been your doing from start to finish and it's you that's walking out of that door now. Just don't you think that when you walk out of that door that you're ever coming back.

DEIRDRE
I won't.
        (slamming the door on her way out)

Reunited with Ken

MIKE PRESSED DEIRDRE to leave Ken and marry him but she wouldn't. Confronted by Ken, Deirdre agreed to give their marriage a second chance. She couldn't leave Ken in the end, and he took her back with open arms, although their marriage would never be quite the same again. Ken booked a holiday for him and Deirdre to Malta and warned Mike off.

Stan and Hilda Ogden celebrate their ruby wedding

Torvill and Dean win gold in the Winter Olympics

Band Aid single recorded

The miners' strike begins

First flight of Space Shuttle *Discovery*

Terminator released

Billy Walker looking good in 1984

BEHIND THE SCENES

When the episode aired with Deirdre ending her affair with Mike and reconciling with Ken, the *Daily Mail* hired the scoreboard at Old Trafford. During a Manchester United vs Arsenal football game the scoreboard lit up with: 'Ken and Deirdre reunited. Ken 1–Mike 0.' There was a huge cheer from the 56,000-strong crowd.

Anne Kirkbride: 'I thought the story would spark off a few fan letters, but I never imagined anything like the press and public reaction we got. It was great stuff – the sort of thing you only get to play once a decade, but I never dreamed it would grip the nation like it did.

On Ken getting physical during his showdown with Deirdre: 'I wasn't prepared for it at all. All of a sudden he grabbed me and I was fighting for my life. I couldn't believe it. I thought he'd gone mad. I was literally fighting to get away from him. I finally managed to free myself and I ran to the other room and I just sat there at the table and started to cry. And there was a camera on me the whole time.

'It's the question you get asked more than any other: "When are you and Ken going to get back together?"'

By the end of the year, Ken and Deirdre were back together and back in love. They attended Stan and Hilda Ogden's fortieth wedding anniversary in the Rovers and Deirdre kissed Ken, asking him if he thought they'd still be together in forty years' time.

1984

Ken has a fling

THE BARLOWS' RELATIONSHIP WAS BACK ON TRACK BUT IT WOULD BE tested once more when infidelity reared its head again. This time it was Ken who was tempted to stray. He'd fallen in love with Sally Waterman, his assistant at the *Weatherfield Recorder*. Deirdre confronted Ken about her suspicions that there was something going on between him and Sally.

Ken denied having an affair but Deirdre called him a liar when he admitted that he fancied Sally and that he'd kissed her. Ken assured Deirdre that all he'd ever done was kiss Sally, just the once. '**Yeah, well, just watch it in future,**' warned Deirdre. '**Keep your eyes on your work!**'

Ken promised Deirdre that kissing Sally Waterman was a one-off, a mistake, and he vowed he'd never leave his wife. However, Sally Waterman would not be the last woman to turn Ken's head during the course of his marriage to Deirdre.

Billy Walker returns and makes a pass at Deirdre

WHEN BILLY WALKER RETURNED FROM JERSEY TO TAKE UP THE REINS at the Rovers, Deirdre mused to Alf in the shop that she'd prefer it if Billy and Ken spent as little time together as possible. '**I don't think they could ever be friendly,**' she said.

''Cos Billy's still got a soft spot for you?' Alf joked. '**He might have got over it, you know!**'

Billy hadn't got over it, however, and he made a pass at Deirdre when he found out that she'd had an affair with Mike. Deirdre turned Billy down flat and told him she didn't want anything to do with him anymore.

Tracy starts asking
awkward questions

1985

Tracy disappears

AT EIGHT YEARS OLD, TRACY STARTED ASKING DEIRDRE SOME awkward questions. She wanted to know why all the other kids at school had their dad's surname. Tracy wondered why her surname was Langton, not Barlow. Deirdre sat down with Tracy and explained all about her dad, Ray, and the divorce. This made Ken start thinking it might be time he legally adopted Tracy.

Tracy then pestered Deirdre for a pet dog and when Deirdre refused, Tracy ran away from home. All on her own she took a train to Newcastle, where she visited Ken's daughter, Susan. Deirdre was hysterical when Tracy went missing, thinking she had been abducted by a stranger. Emily tried to soothe Deirdre and calm her with cups of tea and a sedative. Ken hugged Deirdre but he felt helpless. Deirdre was distraught. She cried so much she had to keep taking off her glasses to wipe her eyes ...

> 'Oh, Tracy, please come back safe and sound. Please, God, don't let anything happen to her, I love her so much. Oh, Tracy.'

Curly Watts and the lads searched down by the canal and found a child's toy but a relieved Deirdre confirmed it wasn't one of Tracy's.

After the train arrived at Newcastle railway station, a man approached Tracy. He asked her if she was lost and offered her a ride in his car. Tracy asked him to go away

GLASSES of '85

Deirdre with Ken's
daughter Susan

and when he didn't, she told him: **'My mummy and daddy told me not to talk to strange people. If you don't go away, I'll tell that policeman on you.'** The man scarpered when he saw a policeman approaching. Tracy was nervous of the police-man herself. When he asked her what she was doing on the platform all on her own, she asked him quietly: **'Am I going to prison?'**

(Oh, if only Tracy had a crystal ball ... She wouldn't be going to prison for another twenty-two years, for the murder of Charlie Stubbs!)

With the help of Bob Peacock, the railway policeman at Newcastle station, Tracy was taken to Susan's house. Deirdre breathed an enormous sigh of relief when the police called to say Tracy had arrived safely in the north-east. Susan brought Tracy back to Weatherfield and ended up moving in to No.1. Ken was overjoyed to have his daughter living with him – until, that is, she announced she'd starting seeing Mike Baldwin.

Ken's family feud with Mike

KEN WAS ABSOLUTELY FURIOUS WHEN SUSAN TOLD HIM SHE AND MIKE were going out with each other. But he knew that no matter how livid he was, he had no option other than to bite his tongue. If Ken wanted Susan to be happy then he had to keep quiet about his daughter dating his bitter rival. He had almost lost Deirdre to Mike and he was determined not to let Mike split up his family again.

Deirdre at work
in the corner shop
offering advice to
Vera Duckworth

Business is booming

Deirdre helped Alf out at the official reopening of the corner shop. Alf improved and expanded Alf's Mini-Market to double its original size.

The Jubilee Years

Deirdre was one of a handful of characters to star in a *Coronation Street* spin-off called *The Jubilee Years*. Alice Hughes (*née* Taylor), an old girlfriend of Ken Barlow's, moved to Australia in 1960. In *The Jubilee Years*, Alice reunited with some major characters as they relived storyline highlights since her departure.

And...

Ken and Deirdre wallpapered the living room at No.1 – in a very exciting pattern of brown and beige stripes.

1986

Ken thumps Mike

BETWEEN WORKING IN THE CORNER SHOP AND BEING MUM TO TRACY, Deirdre did her best to keep the Barlow family together. It wasn't easy, especially as the tension ramped up between Ken and Mike.

Ken tried to cope with the fact that Susan had started going out with his arch-rival Mike but his jealousy became too much. He felt that Mike, unable to take Deirdre away from him, was now taking his daughter instead.

In his anger and frustration, Ken yelled at Deirdre ...

Ken storms into Mike's office where his fury erupts

'It seems to me that all Baldwin has to do is snap his fingers and the women of this household behave like idiotic, infatuated adolescents. I don't understand it. A little weasel like that!'

In his jealousy, Ken told Susan about Mike's affair with Deirdre. If he hoped it would force Susan to split up with Mike he was wrong, and the revelation backfired on Ken. Susan moved out of No.1 and in with Mike, telling Deirdre she hated her for having cheated on her dad. Ken was so incensed when Susan moved out to live with Mike that he stormed round to see Mike at work in Baldwin's Casuals. He pushed his way into Mike's office, not waiting to be invited, telling him: **'I've had enough of your poison in my family. More than enough!'**

Mike tried to answer, but his words were cut short when Ken thumped him hard with a punch that knocked Mike to the floor – in full view of all the factory girls.

Susan marries Mike

THINGS WENT FROM BAD TO WORSE FOR KEN WHEN MIKE PROPOSED TO Susan and she accepted. Adding insult to injury, Ken was stung when Mike announced he would pay for the wedding, denying Ken any involvement in his daughter's big day.

Ken refused to give his blessing to Susan's marriage to Mike. But on the morning of the wedding, Susan's twin brother Peter told Ken some home truths. Peter told his dad that he was in danger of losing Susan for ever if he carried on in his feud with Mike. Despite his bitter feelings against Baldwin, Ken knew he had to do the right thing for his daughter. He raced to the church, arriving just in the nick of time to be at Susan's side to walk her up the aisle and give her away. Tracy followed behind as one of Susan's bridesmaids. Mike was stunned to see Ken at the wedding but Deirdre was over the moon.

There was an awkward pause at the wedding when the vicar reached the point in the ceremony to say: '**If any man can show any just cause why they might not be lawfully joined together, let him now speak or else hereafter hold his peace.**' Although the look on Ken's face gave his true feelings away, he kept quiet as the vicar pronounced his rival and his daughter as husband and wife.

At the wedding reception, Ken looked uncomfortable when he was called to give his father-of-the-bride speech. He started his words with: '**Well, er, this comes as something of a surprise ...**' And although it clearly pained him to say it, he wished Susan and his new son-in-law Mike all the best on their special day.

Tracy becomes a Barlow

SHORTLY AFTER SUSAN'S wedding, Ken gained another daughter when his adoption of Tracy went through. Ken was vetted by Mrs Anderton, the social worker, and she approved Ken as a suitable dad for Tracy. Tracy was now officially a Barlow and Deirdre's family unit seemed secure.

Secretary at **Fairclough & Langton**
The building firm would later be called Fairclough, Langton & Booth, then revert to Fairclough & Langton

Shop Assistant in **Alf's Mini-Market**

1973 **1974** **1975** **1976** **1977** **1978** **1979** **1980** **1981** **1982**

Deirdre

AT WORK

Assistant in **the Kabin**
Deirdre helped out Mavis while Rita was away.

Weatherfield Rainwear
Deirdre quit after she had barely started as Emily didn't feel able to mind Tracy full-time.

Coronation Street Secretarial Bureau
Entrepreneur Deirdre set up the bureau with Emily, working from home.

Shop Assistant in the **Corner Shop**
Alf sold the corner shop to Brendan Scott and its name changed from Alf's Mini-Market to Mr Scott's Provisions. Alf later bought back the shop and reinstalled Deirdre behind the counter.

Part-time **Shop Assistant** in the **Corner Shop** alongside Maureen Holdsworth and Maud Grimes

Factory Manager at **Underworld** working for Mike Baldwin

1993 **1994** **1995** **1996** **1997** **1998** **1999** **2000** **2001** **2002** **2003**

Shop Assistant at **Bettabuys** supermarket

Caretaker
Deirdre worked for Mike Baldwin at Crimea Street flats.

Office Manager at **Sunliners** travel agency
Deirdre worked with Alec Gilroy.

Back at the **Corner Shop**
Deirdre worked for the shop's new owner Dev Alahan as his PA and shop assistant. She stopped working there when Ken found out about her fling with Dev.

1983 **1984** **1985** **1986** **1987** **1988** **1989** **1990** **1991** **1992**

Councillor
Deirdre won the seat as Independent councillor on Weatherfield Council. She stood again in 1991 but lost her seat to Alf Roberts.

Shop Assistant
Deirdre returned to work in Alf's corner shop.

Bettabuys shop assistant, 1994

PA in **Weatherfield Council's Planning Department**
Deirdre lost her job when redundancies were announced and she had to apply for her own job but was unsuccessful.

Helped out at **Barlow's Bookies**

2004 **2005** **2006** **2007** **2008** **2009** **2010** **2011** **2012** **2013** **2014**

Receptionist at **Rosamund Street Medical Centre**

Deirdre is one of the few women on *Coronation Street*
who has never officially worked as a barmaid in the Rovers.

HM the Queen
visits the *Coronation
Street* set, 1982

WHERE'S DEIRDRE?

Coronation Street cast,
Christmas 1981

Coronation Street cast,
2003

1987

Councillor Barlow

DEIRDRE LOVED HER JOB IN THE CORNER SHOP AND SHE LOVED WORKing with Alf. Alf had long been an Independent Weatherfield councillor and would regale Deirdre with his tales from the council chambers. Alf's sense of political fairness resulted in him reporting Ken to the editor of the *Weatherfield Recorder* over claims Ken was using the paper to support the Labour Party.

Deirdre was unhappy with Alf's actions towards Ken and resigned from the corner shop. She handed in her pinny to Alf and left the bacon slicer behind her. Ken then encouraged Deirdre to stand against Alf as an Independent candidate. Deirdre thought Ken was being supportive of her but he was only using her to try to split the Independent vote so that Labour would win.

Deirdre stood against Alf in the Weatherfield elections, energetically campaigning and soon becoming the people's champion. After years of working with her as his assistant, Alf was surprised to find he'd met his political match in Deirdre.

In the local election, Deirdre beat Alf by just seven votes. Alf's defeat ended in him having a heart attack, and his flighty wife Audrey accused Deirdre of nearly killing him.

With her new job and new role Deirdre also decided it was time for a new image. Her long, silky honey-blonde hair had its first flirtation with a perm. This time it was just a demi-wave perm, a precursor to the full-on frizz perm that came later.

Deirdre's passion for her role as Councillor Barlow gave her more confidence and she took on issues and causes for the locals. She campaigned for a road crossing when a child was knocked down on Rosamund Street and helped Emily raise £500 for a local lad to fly to America for a hospital operation.

There was an added energy and vitality to her and it did not go unnoticed by Ken. But instead of being supportive of his wife and proud of her achievements, as Deirdre soared to new heights in her council job, Ken became bitter and jealous. The pressures of council life put a strain on their marriage. When he complained to Deirdre that he was feeling left out, she told him: **'I'm getting a bit tired of all this carping, Ken. Nagging, you'd call it, if the positions were reversed!'**

Ken was furious with Deirdre when she went to a conference in Bournemouth and he wrote an article for the *Weatherfield Recorder*, criticising her for using taxpayers' funds to attend. He even called her a bad mother, making her

BEHIND THE SCENES

Another dimension to Deirdre

Anne Kirkbride was surprised when she was told that Deirdre would become a councillor: 'It was a complete departure which was crazy. I remember Tom Elliott [an ex-*Coronation Street* storyliner and scriptwriter] telling me about it one day. I said, "You're kidding." But it was amazing; in a very short time it suddenly felt right and natural. It was just that I had to get my head round a complete departure like that. It broadened her whole life and outlook and I think it changed her relationship with Ken, because suddenly he couldn't see her as a dim little wife and she was doing something. She became worthy of respect.'

THE REAL WORLD
IN 1987
....
Black Monday
market crash
....
Richard Branson
crosses the Atlantic
in a hot air balloon
....
The Great Storm
levels 15 million
trees and kills 18
....
Terry Waite
kidnapped
....
Fatal Attraction
released
....

feel guilty by saying she was neglecting Tracy, who was hospitalised with appendicitis when a busy Deirdre ignored her symptoms.

Susan leaves Mike

AS KEN HAD PREDICTED, AND SECRETLY WANTED, SUSAN'S MARRIAGE to Mike soon fell apart. She moved back to Newcastle when she found out she was pregnant and told everyone that she'd had an abortion. However, Susan lied and unbeknownst to all she would go on to have Mike's baby – and Ken's grandson – whom she named Adam.

Deirdre offered to collect Susan's belongings from Mike's flat but Ken insisted he do it, wanting to rub salt into Baldwin's wounds. In the flat, Ken spat at Mike about Susan: **'I just wish to God she'd never set eyes on you. I told her when she first met you that you were a load of poison. In future, just stay away from my family!'** and with that, Ken turned and stormed out.

Deirdre enjoys
the perk of Ken's
company car

THE WEATHERFIELD RECORDER

Deirdre invites
Brian Roscoe into her
home

1988

Deirdre imprisoned

DEIRDRE SETTLED WELL IN TO HER ROLE AS A WEATHERFIELD COUNCILLOR
and became self-assured and positive in her dealings with the locals. However, her trust
in one member of the public was badly misplaced when she tried to help a man who
was down on his luck. Brian Roscoe approached Deirdre and said he and his family
were starving as they had no money and he couldn't find a job. Deirdre took on Brian's
cause, much to Ken's annoyance, and he shouted at her: 'You're a councillor, not a
social worker! This is ridiculous … you are getting absolutely ridiculous!'

Ken couldn't understand why Deirdre became so personally involved with Brian's
case. And he was furious with her when she missed Tracy's Christmas pantomime at
school, as she'd invited Brian to visit her at home. Ken told Deirdre she was allowing
council business to dominate her life. Even Tracy started to wonder why her mum was
always at work. 'The world doesn't revolve around little old you all the time, you
know,' Deirdre told Tracy.

'It always revolves around the council,' Tracy sulked.

Undeterred, Deirdre bought Christmas presents for Brian Roscoe's children and
delivered them herself to Brian at home on Christmas Eve. He lived in a flat on the
twelfth floor of Turner House, the kind of high-rise with dirty landings and stinky lifts.
While she was there, it became obvious to Deirdre that Brian was mentally unwell
after he locked himself and Deirdre inside the flat. After a few hours had passed, Ken
reported Deirdre missing to the police, telling them about Brian Roscoe.

Deirdre was terrified at being imprisoned by Brian, especially as it brought back

Brian Roscoe
imprisons Deirdre
in his flat

memories of her attack by the canal all those years ago. She later admitted to Bet Gilroy that she'd feared Brian would rape her. Deirdre cried and pleaded with Brian to let her go, saying Ken would be worried sick and Tracy would be fretting.

But when Brian wouldn't listen to her and kept going on about how bad his life was and how the council hadn't helped him one bit, Deirdre snapped. Her temper flared up and she fought back, yelling at him ...

'I am sick of hearing what you want! You! You! You! You keep moaning and whinging about what you haven't got and what you've never had. Well, hard luck! Take a look at the rest of the world, watch it on your telly. Half the world doesn't know where its next dinner's coming from. This flat? They'd think it was heaven. All right, so it's not but for God's sake, stop moaning and whinging and blaming everybody else! I'm going home!'

'**You're staying here!**' Brian retorted.

'**I am hell as like!**' Deirdre snarled. '**I've had just about enough of you and if you want to stop me, you'll have to kill me!**'

Fired up, Deirdre picked up Brian's portable TV and threatened to throw it out of the window. With Brian distracted and with tears streaming down her face, Deirdre fled from the flat back to safety and Ken.

STREET PEOPLE

Bet Gilroy

GLASSES of '88

Deirdre meets her
arch-nemesis –
Wendy 'flaming'
Crozier

1989

Ken's affair with Wendy Crozier

WITH DEIRDRE CONCENTRATING ON HER CAREER IN THE COUNCIL AND
Ken working all hours to keep the failing *Weatherfield Recorder* afloat, the Barlows
slowly started to drift apart.

Deirdre received a warning at work when confidential reports from council meet-
ings were leaked to the *Weatherfield Recorder*. Her bosses thought that Deirdre was
feeding Ken the reports to print in the paper and they weren't happy with her at all.
However, it wasn't Deirdre who was giving insider information to Ken, it was council
secretary Wendy Crozier.

When Deirdre told Ken that she'd had a ticking-off at work for something that
she hadn't done, he admitted that the mole was Wendy. Deirdre told her boss at the
council about Wendy leaking the stories and Wendy was sacked. Feeling guilty about
Wendy losing her job, Ken took her on as his secretary at the paper – and their pro-
fessional relationship soon blossomed into a full-blown affair that would tear Ken and
Deirdre apart.

Ken and Wendy's affair started as Ken and Deirdre's marriage began to crumble. The affair would last three months before Deirdre confronted him about it on
Christmas Eve. In a highly tense emotional showdown, Ken admitted his affair to
Deirdre. He was sitting in a chair at No.1, having returned home late after spending
the day with Wendy. Deirdre loomed over him, the camera angle giving her the moral
high ground. Framed by her perm and her glasses, Deirdre's face was fierce and furious.

'I want to know where you've been and who with!' she said.

GLASSES of '89

Ken could only manage a quiet '**Oh**' in reply.

She asked him: '**Is it revenge for me and Mike?**'

'**Course not,**' he lied.

'**Is it serious?**' she asked him. '**Answer me, Ken. Is it serious?**'

Ken shifted his gaze – he couldn't look at Deirdre when the final admission came. He couldn't speak. With a simple nod of his head Ken confirmed Deirdre's suspicions.

'**I see,**' she said.

There was a silence and then Ken spoke again: '**The last thing in the world I wanted to do was hurt you.**'

Another silence, and then Deirdre finally spat out the name of Ken's mistress.

'**Wendy Crozier. Am I right?**'

'**Yes.**'

Deirdre stood frozen and then she turned slowly towards their Christmas tree. '**Tree lights seem okay this year,**' she said, without a trace of emotion in her voice. Ken looked as if he hadn't heard her correctly; he'd been expecting a fight from Deirdre. And he was even more puzzled when she said: '**Right, I'm off to bed. Goodnight.**'

Deirdre turned and headed out of the living room but just before she left Ken for the night, she turned back towards him. She wasn't finished with him yet. '**Oh, by the way,**' she said, '**I don't care where you sleep – but it's not in my bed.**' Ken sank back down into his chair and started to cry.

Ken and Deirdre
reach breaking point
in their marriage

No.1
Coronation Street,
home to the Barlows

Deirdre throws Ken out

KEN EXPECTED DEIRDRE TO BE ANGRY AND HURT BY HIS REVELATION, but he was more shocked when her true feelings were revealed. Deirdre told Ken she wasn't going to fight for him to come back, as she didn't think their marriage was worth fighting for. By the end of the year, Deirdre had thrown Ken out of No.1 and decided to file for divorce.

Mike turns sentimental

THE BULLDOZERS MOVED IN TO CORONATION STREET, DEMOLISHING the factory and the community centre. One whole side of the street was cleared to make way for a row of new houses. As the residents watched the buildings being destroyed, Mike and Deirdre shared a quiet moment. Mike turned nostalgic as he and Deirdre watched his factory being knocked down.

'**Nobody understands you, do they?**' she joked.

'**Oh, I don't know. You used to,**' Mike replied.

'**Hey!**' Deirdre said, trying to stop Mike from getting sentimental about their past affair.

'**Oh, I know, I'm not supposed to tell you that,**' he said as he looked at the piles of bricks where his factory once stood. '**But … seeing all this, I'm in the mood for reminiscing.**'

'**Yeah? Well, I'll leave you to it, because I'm not,**' Deirdre replied as she turned and walked away from Mike.

Mike outside his soon-to-be-demolished factory, 1989

1990

Deirdre files for divorce

DEIRDRE AND KEN'S DIVORCE WAS A MESSY AND BITTER PROCESS. It would be a long-drawn-out business, taking almost two years to complete.

Ken sold the *Weatherfield Recorder* to the owner of the *Weatherfield Gazette*, so that he could give Deirdre their home at No.1 in the divorce settlement. He moved in with Wendy Crozier but their relationship didn't last.

However, it wasn't the end of Wendy Crozier in the Barlows' lives. In 2012 Wendy would reappear to cause friction once again.

Deirdre meets handyman Dave Barton

Deirdre dates Dave the handyman

AS A SINGLE MUM ONCE MORE, DEIRDRE STARTED DATING. THE FIRST man she went out with after leaving Ken was handyman Dave Barton. Dave had been passing No.1 when he spotted Deirdre's kitchen ablaze. Tracy had set fire to the kitchen when she was frying chips for Steve and Andy, the McDonald twins, and the chip pan caught fire. Dave rescued Tracy, saved her life and even ended up fitting a new kitchen for Deirdre. What was not to like? Deirdre quickly fell for Dave's easy charms and when they shared their first kiss, Dave pulled her tight to him in a passionate embrace.

Anne Kirkbride and David Beckett met and fell
in love on the set of *Coronation Street* when David
played the role of electrician Dave Barton. Anne and
David married in real life in 1992.

'I've never kissed a councillor before,' he said.

Deirdre replied: 'I was beginning to think you never would.'

Deirdre and Dave grew very close and shared a romantic few days together while Ken and Tracy attended Peter's wedding to Jessica Midgeley in Portsmouth. After six months together, Dave proposed to Deirdre but she rejected his offer of marriage. Dave left Weatherfield and was never seen again.

Deirdre and gangster
Phil Jennings

Deirdre dates Phil the gangster

TRACY HAD PROBLEMS COPING AFTER HER MUM AND DAD SPLIT UP AND she started bunking off school. She was found in the amusement arcade, prompting Deirdre, in her role as councillor, to campaign against schoolkids using the arcades. Deirdre's campaign would bring her into contact with the arcade owner, a man by the name of Phil Jennings, who soon turned Deirdre's head.

Deirdre was single again after Dave had left and she started going out with businessman Phil. He was the owner of PJ Leisure but his business dealings weren't exactly squeaky clean. Unknown to Deirdre, Phil was wanted by the police and local gangsters, and was also a married man. Deirdre had no idea what she was getting herself into, but was impressed when Phil splashed the cash on her in a way that Ken never had.

THE REAL WORLD
IN 1990

Poll Tax riots

Tim Berners-Lee
invents the Internet

West Germany
wins the World
Cup in Italy

The Stone Roses
play Spike Island

Poundland, Netto
and Aldi open their
first UK stores

Phil Jennings warns
Ken to keep away
from Deirdre

Ken tries to commit suicide

WHILE DEIRDRE'S LIFE WAS FILLED WITH NEW RELATIONSHIPS,
Ken became increasingly jealous of his soon-to-be-ex-wife going out with other men.
He begged Deirdre to take him back, many times, and swore undying love for her. But
Deirdre held firm and said she'd never go back to Ken. Events came to a head when
Deirdre started seeing Phil and a jealous Ken stormed into Deirdre's bedroom, looking
for her new man. This led to Deirdre taking out a court injunction to keep Ken away.

On New Year's Eve, Phil took Deirdre to Paris to see in the New Year. At home in
his flat, Ken cooked a meal for Tracy and suggested they take a bottle of champagne
to No.1 to celebrate with Deirdre. Tracy quietly told her dad that Deirdre wasn't there,
that she was in Paris with Phil.

A desperate Ken flew into a rage, demanding to know why Tracy hadn't told him
before. He took out all of his pent-up rage and frustration on Tracy. He yelled at her:
**'So you don't mind your mother going off to Paris for a dirty weekend with some
spiv, do you? You don't see anything wrong with your mother getting in and out
of bed with every man who knocks on the front door?'**

Afraid of Ken's fury, Tracy ran out of his flat and back to No.1. Ken followed and
tried to apologise before Tracy left him and went to stay with a friend. Alone in the
house that used to be his family home, Ken took a bottle of pills and some whisky,
intent on downing the lot. After taking only a few tablets, he was saved by Bet Gilroy
who had entered the house by the back door and found Ken just in the nick of time.

ELSEWHERE IN 1990

Deirdre felt the wrath of her neighbours when she was tempted to sell No.1. Newton & Ridley
offered to buy it so they could expand the Rovers into an American-style bar called Yankees.

While Deirdre was keen to sell, intending to use the money for her and Tracy's future, the residents
set up a campaign to stop the sale going through. Radio Weatherfield backed the campaign and the
Licensed Victuallers Association did battle with the brewery too. In the end, Cecil Newton stepped
in to quash the plans and Deirdre was left feeling contrite.

Ken lends a
sympathetic ear to
Deirdre's problems

1991

Ken gives up on Deirdre

FOLLOWING HIS SUICIDE ATTEMPT, KEN REALISED HE HAD LOST Deirdre for good and agreed to stop hounding her. Ken and Deirdre became friendly again during the course of the year, and their relationship became an even, steady friendship, mostly for Tracy's sake.

Deirdre loses election

DEIRDRE STOOD AGAINST ALF AGAIN IN THE WEATHERFIELD COUNCIL elections. Ken supported Deirdre's campaign and put a 'Vote Deirdre' poster in the window of his flat. But as Ken was living in the flat above Alf's shop, Alf wasn't happy with Ken's show of support and tried to rip the poster down.

Although she had won against Alf at the last election, this time Deirdre lost her seat. She admitted to Mavis in the Kabin that losing her seat on the council came as a bit of shock. **'I did my best, I can't control the way people vote,'** Deirdre moaned. She realised her career in politics was over and soon started looking for another job.

GLASSES of '91

Deirdre *vs.* Alf in the fight for election to the council

Deirdre looks for another job

AS A SINGLE MUM, DEIRDRE NEEDED TO WORK TO KEEP A ROOF OVER her head for her and Tracy at No. 1. When a vacancy came up for a sales representative at Ingram's Textiles, Deirdre applied for it. Mike was surprised to find out Deirdre wanted to work at the factory, and offered her some advice. Over a lunchtime drink in a pub by the canal, Mike had a quiet word with Deirdre about her job application.

He reminded her that they'd been in that same canal pub together in the past during their affair. **'It's quite like old times,'** he cooed. Deirdre told Mike she'd agreed to his offer of a drink for business, not personal, reasons and insisted she wasn't after any

The result of the vote is announced

THE REAL WORLD
IN 1991

Helen Sharman
becomes the first
Briton in space

The Soviet Union
collapses

IRA mortar attack on
10 Downing Street

Freddie Mercury and
Robert Maxwell die

favours from him, saying: 'I can be persuasive, and I'm not afraid to tackle people, I'm not looking for what Percy Sugden calls "a cushy number". I need a job, Mike, a real job. I'm a hard worker. I'm not asking to come onboard for an easy ride. I just want a fair chance, same as anyone else who's after this job.'

Deirdre didn't get the job at the factory. After a brief stint at telesales selling fitted kitchens, Deirdre agreed to work for her latest suitor ...

Deirdre and dodgy Phil

DEIRDRE CONTINUED TO SEE PHIL AND HE PERSUADED HER TO INVEST in his nightclub but she ended up fronting his promotions company instead. She became rather fed up when it was obvious she was doing most of Phil's work. She then started to uncover the seedier side of Phil's life, and found out that he was nothing more than a shady con man who was deep in debt.

Phil disappeared and it was Deirdre who discovered him, badly beaten by a gangster, and about to flee the country with his wife. Deirdre realised what a fool she had been falling for Phil and his flashy lifestyle. But Phil wouldn't be the last con man and fraudster that Deirdre would let into her life.

Dejected Deirdre went back to working with Alf in the corner shop. Once again, she donned her pinny and served the locals from behind the counter. It was a far cry from the powerful world of Weatherfield politics Deirdre had been used to for the last few years.

The corner shop
in 1991

Taking a break from filming the wedding of Liz McDonald and Vernon Tomlin

BEHIND THE SCENES

When Royalty visited the *Coronation Street* set: HRH The Duchess of Cornwall in 2010 ...

... and HRH the Prince of Wales in 2000

Deirdre resists
Tracy's pressure to visit
Ken in hospital

1992

Tracy tries to reunite Ken and Deirdre

KEN WAS ADMITTED TO HOSPITAL WITH A SLIPPED DISC AND WHEN HE was discharged, Deirdre invited him to recuperate at No.1. **'He is still my husband, even if it's not for much longer,'** she explained to Emily.

Liz McDonald was confused as to why Deirdre was taking in Ken just as their divorce was about to be finalised. **'I don't wish to stick my nose in but might it not interfere with your divorce?'** she asked Deirdre.

'I don't know what it'll interfere with,' Deirdre said. **'To be honest, I wish I'd never offered.'** Deirdre had second thoughts about taking her old husband in as her new lodger but, not wanting to let Tracy down, she let Ken move in with them both until he was well.

When the ambulance drew up outside No.1 and Ken was lifted inside by two ambulance men, he greeted Deirdre with: **'It's not the way I ever expected to come back to your front door.'**

Deirdre rolled her eyes and replied: **'It's not the way I did, either!'**

Tracy hoped that having her dad back in the house with Deirdre nursing him, her mum would fall back in love with Ken and they'd reunite. However, nothing was further from Deirdre's mind – her divorce from Ken was finalised during his stay, and the former couple marked the occasion with champagne.

GLASSES of '92

Deirdre and
Ken receive their
decree absolute

Tracy starts to prove a handful for her parents

Trouble with teenager Tracy

KEN STARTED SEEING MAGGIE REDMAN, WHO RAN A FLORIST SHOP, AND Tracy worked at the shop on evenings after school. Deirdre was curious to have a look at Ken's new girlfriend and went to pick Tracy up from the shop one night. Tracy was convinced that her mum was jealous of Ken and Maggie and although Deirdre kept denying that she was, at the same time she kept pumping Tracy for information about Maggie and Ken. Fed up of her mum's questions, Tracy snapped at her …

'You don't care who he's going with, you won't have him back and you don't want to know. But when he is going with someone, you're dead jealous. I suppose you'll try to split them up and everything now, won't you? And you say I'm childish!'

Deirdre told Tracy about Maggie's affair with Mike Baldwin some years earlier, and that Maggie's son Mark was really Mike's son. Mark didn't know who his real dad was and Deirdre made Tracy promise she wouldn't tell Mark. But Tracy couldn't resist spilling the beans and betraying her mum to tell Mark who his real dad was. Maggie was incensed when she found out what Deirdre had done.

THE REAL WORLD
IN 1992

The world's first text message is sent (from Newbury, Berkshire)

Nirvana's *Nevermind* kicks off the grunge explosion

Windsor Castle damaged by fire

Absolutely Fabulous first broadcast

Barcelona hosts the Olympics in Spain

1993

Tracy's history lesson

IN RETALIATION, MAGGIE REVEALED TO TRACY THE BOMBSHELL NEWS about her mum's affair with Mike. Tracy reeled from the discovery about Deirdre and Mike. She and Deirdre argued and Tracy stormed out of the house. When she returned later, Deirdre demanded to know where she'd been but Tracy wouldn't tell her. Tracy wondered why she should be honest when Deirdre hadn't been honest with Ken in the past. Tracy yelled at her mum: **'I suppose you told him you were at a Tupperware party. Or did you tell him you were in bed with Mike Baldwin? Did my dad wait up for you? I bet he did, and I bet you told him a pack of bloody lies. I hate you, you rotten, cowing tart!'**

At that, Deirdre slapped Tracy hard across the face. Their relationship would never be quite the same again.

Deirdre works for Brendan Scott at corner shop

IN THE CORNER SHOP, IT WAS AN END OF AN ERA WHEN ALF RETIRED. Audrey had convinced Alf to sell the shop as she was worried about his health. On his last day in charge, Alf took the bacon slicer home with him as a lasting memento. He was also made an honorary member of the Weatherfield Association of Retail Traders, or WARTs, as they were known.

The shop was sold to Brendan Scott, who renamed it Mr Scott's Provisions and transformed it into an old-fashioned grocery store. Brendan wore a straw boater hat and carried out his deliveries by bike. He employed Deirdre and Emily, forcing them to wear floor-length floral vintage shop dresses complete with starched aprons and frilly caps.

However, Alf's retirement didn't last long, as new owner Brendan had a heart attack and died on the shop floor.

Deirdre weighs up her new boss, Brendan Scott

Deirdre is upset when Debi Scott pays her off, making her unemployed, and sells the stock to Mr Patel

Corner shop blues

IN THE AFTERMATH OF BRENDAN SCOTT'S DEATH, DEIRDRE WAS LEFT to manage the corner shop on her own as best she could. Rita called in one day to ask Deirdre what she was planning to do and if she had thought of looking for another job yet. **'If you offered me a paper round right now, I'd snatch your hand off,'** Deirdre cried, as tears rolled down her face. She mopped her eyes behind her specs and wailed to Rita: **'I can't believe I've got to this age and that's my only option, a shop assistant.'**

Brendan Scott's widow Debi was keen to sell the shop and when it came up for sale, Alf bought it back, much to Audrey's displeasure. Deirdre resigned herself to continuing in her role as Alf's assistant until he sold the shop again, this time to Reg Holdsworth.

Doug Murray turned
Deirdre's head –
and Tracy's

Deirdre and Doug

DOUG MURRAY WAS A CHANCER WHO DRIFTED INTO WEATHERFIELD
when the tax office was chasing him for unpaid bills. He was also a bit of a ladies' man.
As well as dating Deirdre, he flirted with Denise Osbourne and Audrey Roberts.

While Deirdre was going out with Doug, Tracy was in full teenage rebellion mode
and she threw herself at her mum's new man. This was the year that sixteen-year-old
Tracy Barlow turned against her mum. She started drinking and talking back to Deirdre,
having lost all respect for her after the revelation about Deirdre's affair with Mike.

When bankrupt Doug needed a cheque cashed he asked Tracy if she would take
it to the building society to cash it for him. Tracy agreed, on one condition: that if she
cashed the cheque, he would take her out on a date. Deirdre found out about Tracy's
plan and made her give the money back to Doug – and then she promptly dumped
him. Doug disappeared from Weatherfield and Deirdre's life, after stealing Mike
Baldwin's Jaguar. Doug was never seen again and Mike's car was found in Germany.

THE REAL WORLD
IN 1993

Buckingham Palace
opens to tourists

The Space Shuttle
successfully
repairs the
Hubble Telescope

Prince becomes
'The Artist Formerly
Known as Prince'

Jurassic Park
released

Deirdre goes to the florist to look for Tracy but gets quite a shock when she finally finds out who Tracy is now living with

Tracy moves out

TRACY LEFT SCHOOL AT SIXTEEN WITH FOUR GCSEs. AFTER SHE APOLOGISED to Maggie Redman for telling Mark about his real dad being Mike, she started work full-time in the florist shop. It was there she met van driver Craig Lee, who was six years older than her. With so much conflict going on at home with Deirdre, Tracy packed her bags and moved out. Deirdre was stunned when she found out from Maggie that Tracy had moved in with Craig.

Tracy eventually made peace with Deirdre late in the year and moved back in to No.1, bringing Craig too. Deirdre wouldn't let Craig and Tracy share a bedroom and she made Craig sleep in the front parlour. However, it wasn't long before Craig got on Deirdre's nerves as he was lazy and took her hospitality for granted. Deirdre's patience finally snapped with Craig and she asked him to leave – but she was shocked when Tracy moved out with him too.

At the end of the year, Deirdre left Weatherfield and rushed to the Midlands when her mum Blanche had a stroke and Deirdre went to nurse her. Deirdre's absence from the Street would foil a potential Christmas reunion with Ken.

Deirdre has a difficult time when she invites Tracy and boyfriend Craig Lee round for tea

When Deirdre was written out of the show to look after her mum, Blanche, it was because actress Anne Kirkbride had fallen ill. Before Anne left, she had already recorded a love scene with William Roache which was due to air on Christmas Eve, in which Deirdre and Ken kissed. The scene was never transmitted.

Ex-*Coronation Street* producer Sue Pritchard said: 'When Anne Kirkbride had to leave the show through illness, we had to rethink a major storyline which had already been structured and written. It was decided to develop a relationship between Ken and Denise, a woman in whom he had previously shown little interest. The writers made the relationship work and there was terrific chemistry between the two actors.'

Actor Brian Hibbard played Deirdre's boyfriend Doug Murray. He was lead singer of the Flying Pickets, a band who shot to No.1 in the charts in 1983 with their a cappella cover version of Yazoo's 'Only You'.

ELSEWHERE IN 1993

Tracy gave Deirdre a makeover to help her get a barmaid job at the Rovers. Deirdre was upset when Bet told her that she was too old.

1974

Big glasses, big hair, big belts ...
THE DEIRDRE LOOK

1985

DEIRDRE'S GLASSES HAVE BECOME *CORONATION STREET ICONS*. THEY will go down in history as one of the soap's most recognisable props. Throughout Deirdre's life, her glasses have been steamed up with passion, gently washed by tears and have even frosted over, especially when she's been fed up with Ken.

Deirdre was nicknamed 'Miss Sexy Specs' when she was younger. She wore the same style of big glasses for almost thirty years on *Coronation Street*. She removed her glasses for two of her weddings: first at her wedding to Ken in July 1981, and she was specs-free again at her wedding to Samir in 1994.

Vera Duckworth *about* **Deirdre**:

'She could fill a Sunday paper on her own. There's a lot goes on behind them glasses you don't know about.'

Crunch time: Dev smashes Deirdre's big glasses

1995

The glasses

DEIRDRE'S LARGE GLASSES WOULD BECOME HER trademark. That is, until one fateful day in 2001 while working in Dev's corner shop. Deirdre took her glasses off, put them down for just a second on the shop counter and Dev plonked a pile of cardboard boxes – smashing and crushing Deirdre's specs. **'Oh! I knew that was going to happen!'** Deirdre cried to Dev when he tried to apologise. **'Oh no! Look at them! What am I going to do?'**

Deirdre rushed home to get her spare pair. She returned to work wearing them, but they had even bigger frames than the broken ones! Feeling guilty about smashing her glasses, Dev insisted on taking Deirdre to the optician to buy her a new pair, and she traded in her big frames for the final time.

DEIRDRE'S NEW GLASSES IN 2001 WERE HER FOURTH PAIR IN TWENTY-NINE
years on the show. Giving Deirdre a different style of specs made headline news in the
national press and on radio too. Tabloid newspaper readers and *Coronation
Street* fans were given the chance to vote for which glasses
Deirdre would wear on the show.

The glasses chosen by the public had much
smaller frames but it wasn't the end of the big
specs on the Street. In a nod to Deirdre's
glasses from the seventies, Claire Peacock
started wearing big glasses in a similar
style to those which Deirdre had worn.

In 2005 Deirdre's big glasses
made a comic return. When Deirdre
and Bev took Amy to a local safari
park, a gibbon stole the glasses from
her nose. She was forced to hunt in
the attic to find one of her old pairs
with the huge frames to wear until she
visited the optician for a new pair.

During 2014–15, one famous pair
of Deirdre's glasses from the 1970s went
on display at the Coronation Street Tour,
based at the former *Coronation Street* set
on Quay Street in Manchester. Much was
made in the press of the iconic eyewear going
on public display, and they were pictured being
moved from ITV Studios to the Coronation Street
Tour accompanied by a security guard. There, Deirdre's
glasses were signed over and placed inside a secure display unit on the tour. The glasses kept a watchful eye on
other iconic Street props, such as Ena Sharples's hair
net, Hilda Ogden's curlers and Vera
Duckworth's hooped
earrings.

2009

1981

The hair

DEIRDRE'S HAIR HAS GONE THROUGH MANY DIFFERENT STYLES OVER THE YEARS. THE NUM-ber of different hairdos she's had is almost as high as the number of men in her life. And just like her men, some have suited her better than others - while others have done her no favours at all.

Every single one of Deirdre's hairdos tells a story. We only have to look at the different styles of Deirdre with her hair and her glasses and it's likely we'll know exactly what stage she was at in her life – and which man she was with.

From Deirdre's dolly-bird sleek blonde long bob through to the short and practical haircut that she favoured most recently, Deirdre's hair has been long and short, curled and straight.

Her best-known hairdo was the 'Deirdre perm'. It appeared around the same time as Deirdre took on the role of Weatherfield Councillor. She was all about big hair, big specs and even bigger shoulder-pads at that stage. Well, it was the eighties!

But it took a long time for the perm to appear. Deirdre dallied with the long shaggy look of a demi-wave first. Then her hair became shorter and the permed curls tighter.

When Deirdre flew off to Morocco on holiday alone, she sported a much shorter hairdo. And when she wed Samir, her hair was shorter still.

It would then grow out beautifully into the style we remember Deirdre for, the short and practical look she maintained for the remainder of her life.

1987

1990

Deirdre's perm
taking shape

2000

Anne Kirkbride: 'What I do every so often is I go through my wardrobe and things I still quite like but am not likely to wear again, I pass them on to Deirdre. I'll go out and I'll buy something and I'll wear it and I don't feel right in it and I think, "Why? What is it about this?" and it suddenly dawns on me that it's a Deirdre dress so I take it in to wardrobe and I go, "I've done it again, I've bought another Deirdre dress," and they go, "Great!" and it goes on Deirdre's rail.'

Deirdre's belt as shock absorber! Tracy tells Deirdre and Ken she is pregnant, 2011

Deirdre's belt starring when James and Tracy argue and Deirdre tries to calm them down

The belts

IF THERE WAS A SIGNATURE ITEM THAT DEIRDRE MADE HER OWN, it was her chain belt. It first made an appearance as part of Deirdre's wardrobe in the late 1970s and has been a firm favourite ever since. She even started online shopping to buy more belts.

Happy again —
Deirdre and Samir

1994

Trying times for Deirdre

DEIRDRE RETURNED HOME AFTER NURSING MUM BLANCHE AND FOUND herself a new job in Bettabuys, the local supermarket, She hoped to repair her relationship with Ken and was happy to see him, eager to put the past behind her and pick up the pieces again. However, Ken had shock news for Deirdre. Not only had he started a fling with hairdresser Denise Osbourne while Deirdre had been away, but Denise was pregnant with Ken's baby!

Deirdre was furious with Ken and very upset, especially after all the times she had begged Ken to have a child of their own. She refused to keep Ken and Denise's baby news a secret, as Ken had asked her. In a fit of temper in the Rovers, she blurted out the news to the stunned customers in the pub.

After her outburst in the Rovers, Deirdre felt humiliated and needed to get away from Ken and Denise. She decided to fly off on holiday alone, to Agadir in Morocco. When she announced her exotic holiday plans in the Rovers, Betty told her a change of scene was maybe just what she needed: **'Two weeks of sun, sea and sheep's eyes!'**

Deirdre meets Moroccan toy-boy

WHILE SHE WAS IN MOROCCO, DEIRDRE HAD A HOLIDAY ROMANCE WITH a twenty-one-year-old called Samir Rachid. Samir worked as a waiter in the three-star hotel where Deirdre stayed on her package holiday. She would return to Weatherfield with more than a suntan and a few souvenirs when her toy-boy lover followed her home.

Deirdre had fallen in love with Samir, despite being almost double his age. She asked Emily to lend her money, which she sent to Samir so that he could fly over from Morocco. She had expected Emily to disapprove of the request if she knew what it was for, and so she wasn't entirely honest with her about the reason for the loan.

When Samir arrived on the Street, Deirdre was overjoyed. She only intended for him to come over for a holiday but he was so desperately in love with Deirdre that he let his plane fly home without him and stayed on with her instead. Deirdre's friends thought she was mad for letting Samir into her life. They told her she was making a fool of herself over a toy-boy lover that she barely knew. Deirdre blissfully ignored them all.

Samir introduced Deirdre to exotic food, cooking her a lamb tagine with couscous for her tea. **'It should be cooked on charcoal,'** he explained.

'It's hard to get round here, is charcoal,' Deirdre noted.

Samir started work as a waiter in the Casablanca, a local Moroccan restaurant, but as he didn't have a work permit the immigration officials started sniffing around. They accused Samir of having duped Deirdre into bringing him into the country and even talked about deportation. Deirdre knew there was only one way for her to keep Samir in the country legally and that was by marrying him. She knew that if she wed Samir, it would prove to her friends, and Ken, how serious she was about Samir, that he wasn't the joke toy boy that they all thought he was.

Wedding to Samir Rachid

DEIRDRE'S PROPOSAL TO SAMIR WAS MORE PRACTICAL THAN ROMANtic. She popped the question as they were both doing the dishes in the kitchen at No.1. Deirdre was drying the plates as Samir washed the pots, wearing rubber gloves. He didn't reply to Deirdre's proposal immediately; he thought about it carefully over the next few days, keeping Deirdre on tenterhooks before he finally accepted.

Deirdre's wedding to Samir was a bittersweet affair. Deirdre's oldest friend Emily refused to attend, as she felt Deirdre was making a fool of herself. Ken accused Samir of marrying Deirdre to get a British passport, and said he wanted nothing to do with the pair of them. Tracy turned up for her mum's wedding, but she sat at the back of the register office looking pained and then stormed out in disgust. It seemed the only two people who approved of Deirdre and Samir being married were the happy couple themselves.

At the service, the registrar pronounced Deirdre and Samir as husband and wife. Samir slipped the ring onto Deirdre's finger and asked: **'I may kiss her now?'**

'You most certainly can,' the registrar replied.

Samir moved in to No.1 with Deirdre and they soon settled into a pattern of domesticity. Samir even learned how to cook a Lancashire hotpot and started drinking beer in the Rovers. When the newly married couple popped in to the pub for a drink, Deirdre told Bet that Samir had landed himself a new job in a Spanish restaurant in town.

'Well, it'll get you out of house, won't it? Give you a bit of time away from t'wife,' Bet joked.

Samir didn't see the funny side of her comment. **'I don't want any time away from Deirdre. I want to be with her the rest of my life,'** he said.

Bet went all dewy-eyed and sighed to Deirdre: **'It's a different culture, in't it?'**

Deirdre just smiled, glanced at Samir and nodded her head.

The tension mounts in the Rachid household as Tracy struggles with her kidney problems

The immigration officials hadn't finished with Samir, however. Even after Deirdre and Samir were wed, he was threatened with deportation after the officials were certain that their marriage was a sham. Concerned they would be separated for ever if this happened, Samir told Deirdre he was going home to Morocco. Deirdre was shocked when he said that he expected her, as his wife, to return with him too. **'Deirdre! I'm your husband!'** he asserted, but she gave back as good as she got: **'Hey! Now don't start saying the little woman has to do as she's told just because you're the man!'**

Samir apologised and although Deirdre was adamant that she wouldn't go to live in Morocco, she finally softened and changed her mind. **'You're right,'** she told him. **'There's nothing for us here. I'll go with you wherever you want, whenever you want, just as long as we're together.'**

Deirdre and Samir left for Morocco, with Deirdre selling No.1. The house that had once been Ken Barlow's family home was now in the hands of a new owner – Ken's arch-rival, Mike Baldwin. Ken would buy the house back from Mike after a few months.

However, after only a short time into their new lives abroad, Deirdre and Samir were called back to Weatherfield by a family emergency.

Ken and Deirdre unite in their concern for Tracy. Samir Rachid feels excluded

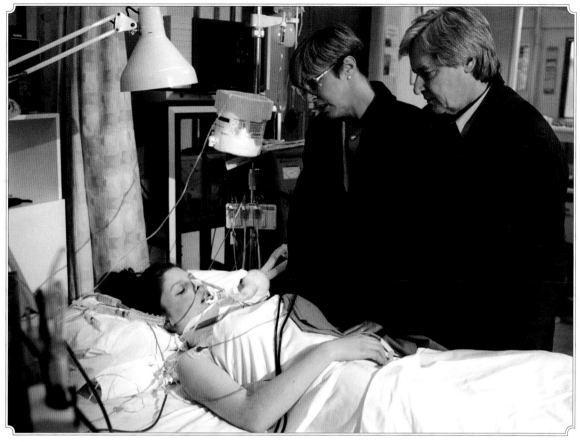

Tracy in hospital with
kidney failure after
taking ecstasy at a club

1995

Samir dies

DEIRDRE FLEW BACK FROM MOROCCO TO BE WITH TRACY, WHO WAS IN hospital in a drug-induced coma after she'd taken a bad ecstasy tablet. Samir, unable to live without Deirdre by his side, returned with her. With Ken and Deirdre united in their despair over Tracy, Samir started to feel left out of Deirdre's life while she and Ken bonded again.

Tracy had suffered severe kidney damage and needed a kidney transplant. Deirdre and Ken were tested to see if they were compatible, but neither of them were a suitable match. Samir finally saw his chance to do something for Deirdre – he was tested too and found to be a perfect match. As Samir walked to the hospital for the transplant operation, he followed the route along the canal. A group of youths pushed past him, one of them making a racist remark. Later that evening, Deirdre waited by the phone for a call from Samir to tell her how his operation had gone, when two police officers arrived at her door.

Stunned, Deirdre took in the news that Samir was in hospital with serious head injuries he'd sustained by the canal. She rushed to the hospital but was told that Samir would not regain consciousness. In her grief, Deirdre agreed that his kidney could be removed to save Tracy's life. **'Goodbye, angel,'** wept Deirdre as Samir's body was wheeled into the operating theatre.

THE REAL WORLD
IN 1995

Radiohead release
The Bends

Nick Leeson
jailed for Barings
Bank collapse

Princess Diana
admits her affair
with James Hewitt

Space Shuttle
Atlantis docks with
the Soviet Union's
Mir space station

Toy Story released

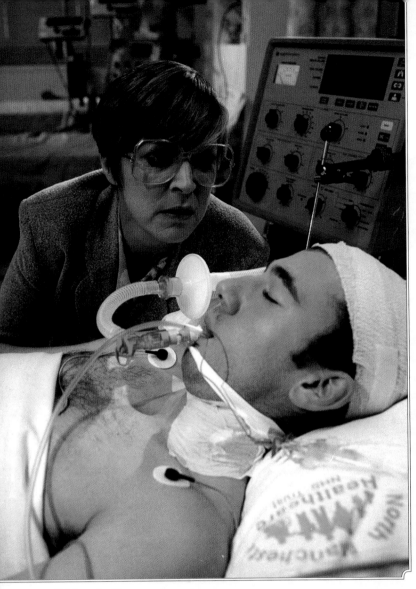

Deirdre at Samir's bedside in hospital

Tracy's operation went well, although Deirdre blamed her daughter for Samir's death. When Deirdre went to see Tracy to tell her that Samir was dead, Tracy was asleep in her hospital bed. Deirdre had a bunch of flowers in her hand, and she flung them down angrily onto Tracy's bed and stormed out. It was left to Ken to tell Tracy that Samir had died and he told her that she mustn't blame herself for what had happened. Tracy replied that she didn't blame herself, she blamed Ken.

Deirdre had the harrowing task of accompanying Samir's body back to his family in Morocco. Later in the year, supported by Ken and Liz, Deirdre went to the inquest of Samir's death, where an open verdict was recorded.

Deirdre as a widow

WHEN DEIRDRE RETURNED HOME FROM MOROCCO AS A WIDOW to Weatherfield, it was Mike Baldwin who took care of her. He offered her a flat in his new development at Crimea Street, along with the job of caretaker for the block of flats.

One of the other residents in the flats seemed a little odd to Deirdre. He was called Roy Cropper, and he always carried a shopping bag that had his door key attached to it by a string. Deirdre thought Roy was an oddball, but in her mourning and grief over losing Samir, she didn't pay him too much heed. She locked herself away and kept herself to herself, crying over Samir's death.

However, it was Roy who noticed that Deirdre's milk hadn't been taken in from her doorstep and when he knocked on her door, he worried when she didn't answer. Roy called Mike Baldwin to tell him he was concerned about Deirdre. Mike called round to see her and Deirdre explained to Mike how much she missed Samir. Deirdre broke down and wept in the arms of her old friend Mike.

1996

Deirdre and Ken reunite – briefly

WHEN KEN SPLIT UP WITH Denise Osbourne – after he found out she'd been seeing another man behind his back – Deirdre was the one who consoled him. Deirdre even agreed to babysit Ken and Denise's son, Daniel, while Ken was at the theatre one night. When he returned home, he and Deirdre shared a late-night drink and confided to each other that they were both lonely. Not only that, they admitted that they had no one else in the world they could confide in apart from each other.

The two of them started enjoying each other's company again and

Ken and Deirdre back together again

a reconciliation looked like it was on the cards. Deirdre was happy to be getting back together with Ken, but she hadn't reckoned on Ken's ever-wandering eye and what would happen next.

Working at Sunliners

WHEN SHE FELT THAT THE WORLD OF WORK WAS PASSING HER BY, Deirdre decided to start looking for another job. She applied for an office job at Baldwin's factory but was hurt to be spurned by Mike in favour of another candidate.

She registered with a temping agency and while waiting for her first assignment, found herself in Sunliners Travel Agency, owned by Alec Gilroy. She had called in to book herself on a coach trip to London and while she was there, Alec mentioned that he was looking for someone to work full-time. Deirdre jumped at the chance of working there with Alec, and the ex-theatrical agent hired her on the spot. **'I'm supposed to ask whether you can use a VDU,'** he told her, **'but I'd much rather ask if you can tap-dance!'**

GLASSES of '96

Tracy marries Robert Preston

FULLY RECOVERED FROM HER STROKE, DEIRDRE'S MUM BLANCHE returned to Weatherfield for Tracy's wedding to Robert Preston. On the morning of the wedding, Blanche sat with Deirdre and Tracy at No.1 as Deirdre tried to hurry Tracy into getting dressed for her big day. Blanche reminded Deirdre that on her wedding day to Ray, she was just as laid-back as Tracy was now.

'I had palpitations!' Deirdre joked. 'I ought to know.'

''Spose you ought, you've done it often enough!' sniped Tracy to her thrice-wedded mum.

Tracy was wed in a green crushed-velvet dress and a pair of blue boots, and wore green varnish on her nails. When the best man failed to show up with the wedding ring, Tracy asked Deirdre if she could have Samir's ring from her finger to wear.

'I promised his memory that I'd never take it off,' mourned Deirdre.

Ken nodded sagely and said: 'Considering what he has given her, I think he'd let it go.'

Deirdre handed Samir's ring to Tracy and the wedding went ahead. After their wedding, Tracy and Robert moved to London.

Deirdre's first date as a widow

DEIRDRE BRIEFLY DATED AUDREY ROBERTS'S SON, STEPHEN REID, when he flew in from Canada to see his mum. Mike invited Deirdre out to dinner with him, his wife Alma and Stephen. He did it just to make Alma jealous, knowing that she had feelings for Stephen.

Deirdre and Stephen hit it off, and when Stephen returned to the UK later that year, he and Deirdre went on a date in the Rovers – her first since Samir had died. But their date led nowhere as Stephen went back to Canada without asking Deirdre out again. Deirdre felt that Stephen only asked her out in the first place to be polite and that he thought she was too old for him.

ELSEWHERE IN 1996

Good neighbour

Deirdre offered her flat in Crimea Street as a refuge for Liz McDonald when she was the victim of domestic abuse at the hands of her ex-squaddie Irish husband, Jim. Deirdre's neighbour, single mum Tricia Armstrong, and her son Jamie were also given support and a safe haven by Deirdre in her flat when social services tried to take Jamie away.

1997

Deirdre dumps Ken

DEIRDRE AND KEN WERE SEEING EACH OTHER AGAIN, BUT WHILE WORKING at Weatherfield Comprehensive, Ken became a bit too friendly with the headmistress, Sue Jeffers. After the head had kept Ken on at work while redundancies were being made, Sue developed a crush on Ken. He tried to shrug it off but it got out of hand, and after an argument with Deirdre, Ken took Sue for a drink and then invited her back to No.1. A little later, Deirdre let herself into the house, only to walk in and find Ken with Sue Jeffers – in bed! Ken knew he had gone too far and that Deirdre would never forgive him this time. He was right – Deirdre promptly dumped Ken, again.

THE REAL WORLD
IN 1997

Channel 5 launched

First *Harry Potter* book published

Tony Blair's New Labour take power

Princess Diana dies

Teletubbies first broadcast

Deirdre meets Jon the fake pilot

Deirdre and Jon Lindsay

LIFE WAS GOING WELL FOR DEIRDRE. She was promoted to manageress at Sunliners and moved in to a flat over Skinner's bookies. While at a singles night with Maureen Holdsworth in town, she met handsome airline pilot Jon Lindsay.

They started dating and Deirdre was wined and dined in style by Jon, who lavished gifts on her. She was smitten with him, wowed by his pilot's uniform and his tales of jetting all over the world. However, he was spinning Deirdre a web of lies in which she would become dangerously entangled.

Not only was Jon married with children and stringing Deirdre along by the heartstrings, he was a fantasist and a con man involved in identity fraud and financial deception. Jon had also lied about

Jon the fake pilot —
and Deirdre believed
every word

Deirdre confronts Jon
in the airport tie-shop

being a pilot – he really worked in a tie shop at Manchester airport. It was Ken who spotted Jon working in the shop and he revealed what he'd seen to Deirdre. She thought Ken was lying to her but he told her straight: **'Have you seen him actually flying planes? Because I've seen him actually selling ties!'**

Deirdre confronted Jon and he admitted he had lied to her about being a pilot, saying he could no longer fly after suffering dizzy spells. Deirdre's specs must have been rose-tinted at this point because she forgave him after he promised he loved her – and then he asked her for cash.

Deirdre handed over £5,000 to use as a deposit on a posh house in Didsbury and Jon gave her a gold credit card to use to her heart's content. He popped the question to a delighted Deirdre and they threw a joint engagement and house-warming party. Deirdre was so happy with Jon, her new home, her new life. Nothing could spoil it for her now, could it?

Outside the court
room, waiting to go
on trial

1998

Free the Weatherfield One

GLASSES of '98

DEIRDRE JUMPED IN A TAXI ONE NIGHT WITH A BOTTLE OF CHAMPAGNE in the hope of surprising Jon at home. But the surprise was on Deirdre when she turned up to find him with his wife and kids. Realising she'd been duped, Deirdre went straight to the bank to withdraw the money from their joint account that she'd given Jon – and that's when she was arrested for fraud! Jon had cleverly ensured that the credit card, mortgage and bank account were all in Deirdre's name, not his.

The trial was big news in Weatherfield. Deirdre's friends and neighbours rallied around her, giving her every support. Emily was certain that Deirdre was innocent. She entered the witness box in court as part of Deirdre's defence and said: **'If Deirdre's guilty of these preposterous allegations then ... I'm a banana!'**

Deirdre and Jon
in court awaiting
sentence

Residents protest
Deirdre's innocence
outside the court

Ken was called to testify against Deirdre in the trial after he admitted to the police that he knew Jon wasn't actually a pilot. He'd kept quiet about the secret at first as he didn't want to hurt Deirdre. When Mike found out that Ken had been called as a witness for the prosecution, he called him treacherous and warned him: **'If Deirdre goes down, it's because of you, Barlow!'** Mike was as certain of Deirdre's innocence as Emily was. He put his solicitor, Frances Stillman, on the case and paid Deirdre's legal fees for her.

However, the jury in court thought differently. Presented with the evidence, a shocked Deirdre was found guilty. Jon's defence team made Deirdre appear to be the brains behind his mortgage fraud and credit card scams. He was given a six-month suspended sentence and poor Deirdre was given eighteen months in jail.

Terrified Deirdre
in court

THE REAL WORLD
IN 1998

Good Friday
Agreement signed

Hosts France win
the World Cup

Angel of the North
sculpture opened

The Weatherfield One

Deirdre and cell mate
Jackie Dobbs queue in
the prison canteen

The judge summed up the jail sentence to Deirdre, ending with: '**You are clearly the orchestrator of this serious fraud. You ensnared a vulnerable married man and cruelly and systematically exploited him for your own material gain. I have no option but to pass on you a custodial sentence. Have you anything to say?**'

And that's when Deirdre broke down and cried: '**I didn't do any of it!**'

A distraught Deirdre was taken down to the cells, in shock and unable to speak. When she was moved to the prison, she was greeted by a nasty piece of work in the shape of prison officer Veitch, who would make Deirdre's life hell while she was in jail.

BEHIND THE SCENES

Deirdre's courtroom drama and jail sentence resulted in one of the biggest responses to a storyline the show had ever had. The campaign to Free the Weatherfield One was launched and would run until Deirdre was freed.

Fact and fiction became blurred over Deirdre's miscarriage of justice and the campaign gathered momentum. The newspapers went wild with the Free the Weatherfield One campaign. The tabloids gave away 'Free Deirdre' T-shirts and stickers as Deirdre's dilemma gripped the nation.

Even Prime Minister Tony Blair became involved. In the fun spirit of the campaign, he promised to intervene to free Deirdre from jail, saying he would instruct Home Secretary Jack Straw to look into her case.

Anne Kirkbride found herself at the centre of the show's biggest storyline. She said: 'I still have trouble getting my head around how big it got. It was mad. I remember my mother-in-law rang me up and said, "Put the telly on, you're on the *News at Ten* – you've been mentioned by Tony Blair!" It all became incredibly surreal and I did just want to say, "Look, it's not real, surely there are more important causes to be campaigning for?"'

When Deirdre was finally freed, the storyline made front-page headlines.

Settling into prison life
with cell mate Jackie

'**Hello, Deirdre,**' Veitch said, sarcastically. '**Welcome to your new home.**'

With Mike and Emily working tirelessly to clear Deirdre's name, Mike even offered to pay for a retrial. Deirdre would spend only three weeks in prison, sharing her cell with violent Jackie Dobbs. She was finally freed when another of Jon Lindsay's women came forward to confirm how much of a con man he was. Jackie Dobbs followed Deirdre back to Weatherfield and even moved in with her for a while.

As Deirdre walked free from the prison, who should she see being brought in, handcuffed, but Jon Lindsay. '**You should like it in there, Jon,**' Deirdre shouted. '**It's directly under the flight path to the airport.**'

Celebrating Deirdre's
release in the Rovers

Deirdre's
MEN

ALTHOUGH KEN WAS DEIRDRE'S ALMOST-CONSTANT COMPANION, THERE WERE MANY MORE men in her life. Most notable was her affair with Mike Baldwin and her one-night stand with shop-keeper boss Dev Alahan. But there have been other marriages, broken engagements and drunken snogs in Deirdre's life. Let's have a look back at the men that Deirdre loved and lost …

1972 Jimmy Frazer

Deirdre's first scene in 1972 saw her seated in a pub drinking with Jimmy Frazer. He was her first ever date.

Ray in 1976

Billy in 1973

1974-5 Billy Walker

Engaged to be married before Deirdre called it off.

1974 Maurice Gordon

Late night with oil-rigger Maurice. Blanche slapped Deirdre over her loose morals. Ray Langton told him to back off.

1975-8 Ray Langton

They wed in 1975 and in 1977 Deirdre gave birth to their baby daughter, Tracy. After Ray had an affair with waitress Janice Stubbs, Deirdre left him and Ray moved to the Netherlands. They were divorced in 1980. Ray returned in 2005 and died on Deirdre's second wedding day to Ken.

1978 Tim Gibbs

Deirdre met an old admirer, Tim Gibbs, who was very interested to learn that she was separated from Ray.

Deirdre and **Tim** in 1978

Mike in 1979

1979   Billy Walker

Deirdre dated Billy a second time. She declined Billy's offer of a new life in Jersey.

1979   Mike Baldwin & Ken Barlow

Deirdre dated both Mike and Ken. She chose Ken and went on holiday with him to the Lake District.

1980   Jeff 'Fangio' Bateman

Deirdre went out on one date with Jeff. He was one of the first customers at the Coronation Street Secretarial Bureau she ran with Emily Bishop.

1980   Alan Skidmore

Deirdre went on one date with Alan, who worked as Mike Baldwin's sales manager in London. Alan wasn't keen when Deirdre brought toddler Tracy on their date.

1981   Dirk van der Stek

Deirdre dated Ray's business colleague Dirk the Dutchman.

1981   Ken Barlow & Mike Baldwin (again)

Deirdre dated both Ken and Mike and chose Ken over Mike, again. She married Ken on 27 July. (They divorced in 1992.)

1982–3   Mike Baldwin

When married life to Ken became a drudge, Deirdre spiced things up with an affair with Mike. The affair climaxed with the infamous love triangle.

Ken in 1976

Deirdre and Dave in 1990

Mike Baldwin

Deirdre agreed to a date with Mike but walked out when it became clear he was only trying to rile Ken and Alma.

1992-3 Doug Murray

Doug was a chancer and a drifter. Deirdre dumped him after Tracy made a pass at him.

Doug in 1992

1994-5 Samir Rachid

Deirdre married Samir, the Moroccan waiter she met on holiday in Agadir. He died after donating his kidney to Tracy.

Samir in 1994

1990 Dave Barton

Handyman/electrician who saved Tracy's life. Dave proposed to Deirdre but she turned him down.

1990-91 Phil Jennings

Deirdre took up with local gangster and con man Phil. He fled the country with his wife after being beaten up by heavies.

Phil in 1991

1996 Stephen Reid

Deirdre briefly dated Audrey's son Stephen when he flew in from Canada to visit his mum.

1996-7 **Ken Barlow** (again)

Deirdre and Ken had a very brief reunion

Jon in 1997

1997-8 **Jon Lindsay**

Deirdre fell for con man and fantasist Jon Lindsay. He proposed and she accepted but his lies saw her end up in prison for fraud.

1999-2015 **Ken Barlow** (again)

Deirdre and Ken were reunited. They remarried on 8 April 2005.

2001 **Dev Alahan**

Deirdre fell for her shopkeeper boss and they had an ill-advised one-night stand on Christmas Day.

2006 **Man in a pub**

On a girls' night out in the Weatherfield Arms, Deirdre snogged a man she knew from work at the council. He ended up blackmailing her.

Deirdre and **Lewis** in 2010

2010 **Lewis Archer**

Deirdre and Lewis's kiss was caught on CCTV in the bookies' shop.

Dev in 1999

〔127〕

Ken and Deirdre
dance a tango at the
Valentine's Disco in
the Flying Horse

1999

Deirdre and Ken reunite – again

DEIRDRE'S MUM BLANCHE RETURNED TO LIVE IN WEATHERFIELD AND soon set about trying to get Deirdre back together with Ken. She sent Deirdre and Ken the same Valentine card, hoping each of them would think the card had come from the other. They knew what she was up to, and Deirdre accused Blanche of interfering in her life. However, Blanche's tactics did bring Deirdre and Ken closer as they united in despair over her matchmaking skills.

Then Tracy returned to Deirdre's life briefly after she split with husband Robert. As Deirdre and Ken helped Tracy through her marriage problems, they became closer still. Heartened by this, Blanche threw a sixtieth birthday party for Ken, telling him: '**It's a milestone, not a tombstone. Today you're going to have fun,**' and the Barlows were at last reunited and back together again.

Audrey noticed the smile on Deirdre's face when she was out with Ken and told her: '**You look like summat out of a Catherine Cookson.**' Audrey then commented to Rita that Ken and Deirdre had a lot of mileage between them. Rita sagely replied: '**Mileage doesn't count – it's destination that matters.**'

As a reunited couple, Deirdre and Ken attended Roy Cropper and Hayley Patterson's wedding. When Hayley threw her bridal bouquet into the small crowd of guests at their wedding in Roy's Rolls, Deirdre caught it squarely, much to everyone's delight – and Deirdre's surprise. '**I can recommend a very good vicar,**' Roy told her.

E L S E W H E R E   I N   1 9 9 9

Ken started work as a supermarket trolley collector at Frescho and wore his name badge labelled 'Kenny' with pride. Deirdre was less than impressed with Ken's new role and told him: '**I'm not sharing my bed with a trolley dolly!**'

THE REAL WORLD
IN 1999

Paddington
rail crash

Gary Glitter
and Jonathan
Aitken jailed

David Beckham
marries
Victoria Adams

Prince Edward
marries
Sophie Rhys-Jones

Britney Spears
releases her
debut album

2000

Deirdre meets her Waterloo

THE RESIDENTS OF *CORONATION STREET* CELEBRATED THE MILLENNIUM with a party on the cobbles. A stage was set for entertainment and an Abba tribute band, Fabba, made up of the Underworld girls, was assembled ready to belt out some hits for the crowd. But just before the band was due to perform, Gwen Loveday took ill and had to pull out. Desperate for a new band member at short notice, Hayley asked Deirdre if she would step into the breach. Not one to let the team down, Deirdre donned a feather boa and a glitter wig. She got on the stage and danced and sang alongside Linda Sykes, Janice Battersby and Hayley Cropper.

Blanche was in full fancy dress with a basket of fruit piled high on her head as Carmen Miranda as she turned to ask Ken: **'Is that Deirdre up there? What on earth does she look like … at her age!'**

Blanche dressed up as Carmen Miranda for the Millennium party

GLASSES of 2000

Mr and Mrs

DESPITE HER ACID TONGUE, BLANCHE'S HEART WAS IN THE RIGHT place and she wanted nothing more than for Deirdre and Ken to be married again. When a 'Mr and Mrs' competition was announced in the Rovers, Blanche told Deirdre that Ken had put their names down to enter. She then told Ken that Deirdre had entered their names. When Deirdre found out what her mother was up to, she refused to take part and Ken took Deirdre out for dinner instead. When the compère called Deirdre and Ken to take part in the quiz, Blanche shouted: **'They're not here. And they're not even married!'** The competition was won by Roy and Hayley Cropper.

Deirdre returns to work at the corner shop

AFTER TWO YEARS WORKING AS MIKE'S OFFICE MANAGER AT Underworld, Deirdre found herself unemployed once more. Ken had started a new job, writing a weekly column for the *Weatherfield Gazette*. When one of the women working at Mike's factory complained to Ken about the conditions there, Ken wrote a scathing column in the paper attacking Mike. Mike was incensed. He assumed that Deirdre had given Ken the insider information and promptly sacked her. Deirdre was furious with Ken for not revealing the source of the story, which could have meant her keeping her job.

In need of work, Deirdre started to help Dev Alahan in the corner shop. She worked as shop assistant and Dev's PA and helped him sort out his life. Dev was very grateful indeed for her help. **'The gods have directed you here,'** he drawled.

'No they haven't,' replied Deirdre. **'It was my mother – we're out of cornflakes.'**

Deirdre starts working for Dev in the corner shop

THE REAL WORLD
IN 2000

First UK broadcast
of *Big Brother*

Millennium Bridge
opens — and closes

A shower of
sprats falls on
Great Yarmouth

Gladiator released

50 Cent shot nine
times in Queens, NY

Australia hosts the
Olympics in Sydney

Blanche wasn't at all happy about Deirdre working in the shop. She thought it was well beneath her daughter's capabilities. But in the same way that Deirdre had once taken control at Fairclough & Langton's builder's yard in the past, she now took control of the bills and paperwork at Alahan's. Dev was impressed with Deirdre's work and offered her promotion and a pay rise.

Deirdre was happy in her new job and her life with Ken. When they attended Curly and Emma Watts's wedding together late in the year, Deirdre would once again catch the bride's bouquet. Surely nothing could spoil her happiness now ... could it?

2001

Deirdre blabs big baby secret

GLASSES of 2001

KEN'S DAUGHTER SUSAN RETURNED TO WEATHERFIELD WITH A SECRET. When Susan left husband Mike thirteen years earlier, she had told Mike that she had had an abortion. On her return she confided to dad Ken that this had been a lie. Away from Mike, she had gone through with the pregnancy and had given birth to a son, Adam, who was now twelve years old.

Ken reeled from Susan's shock news, and struggled to come to terms with the fact he was grandfather to the son of his bitter rival Mike. Susan pleaded with Ken never to break the news to Mike and Ken promised that he would carry the secret to his grave. But he did tell Deirdre … and that's when the baby secret exploded and almost blew the Barlows' world apart.

Deirdre couldn't contain herself with such a major piece of family gossip and shared it with Dev in the corner shop. Dev strongly felt that Mike should know about his secret son and decided to tell him. The family fall-out over the Barlow–Baldwin baby backfired spectacularly on Deirdre. She received a harsh telling-off from Ken and the two of them fell out, again.

THE REAL WORLD
IN 2001

First episode of
The Office broadcast

Britain and USA
begin airstrikes
in Afghanistan

Tony Blair's Labour
government
re-elected

*Harry Potter and
the Philosopher's
Stone* released

Deirdre and Ken split up and make up

AFTER SUSAN DIED IN A CAR CRASH, KEN DECIDED TO DO WHAT HE thought best for his grandson. He took on Mike and fought him for custody of Adam. Ken's solicitor stressed the importance of a stable background and family home for Adam, and that's when Ken asked Deirdre to marry him. Ken and Deirdre were under no illusions about his proposal. They both knew that Ken wanted a marriage of convenience, not romance. Ken had asked for Deirdre's hand in marriage for purely selfish reasons to get one over on Mike in his battle over Adam. It came as no surprise to Ken when Deirdre turned him down flat.

Deirdre was less than impressed with Ken's proposal but there was worse to come as Ken's battle with Mike over Adam ramped up. Ken decided, without consulting Deirdre, that he was moving to live in Scotland and he was taking Adam with him. Deirdre was incensed with Ken, packed her bags and moved out. In tears, she waited at the bus stop for the Weatherfield Wayfarer just as Dev drove past. He offered her a

Ken listens to old
friend Alma Halliwell

lift in his car and when he found out what had happened, offered her his spare room to stay in until things calmed down at home.

It didn't take long before Ken, prompted by Alma to look into his heart, turned up on Dev's doorstep to beg Deirdre to come home.

'**We can get past this**,' Ken told her.

'**Oh, Ken,**' cried Deirdre, and she moved back to No. 1.

Deirdre and Dev

MEANWHILE, IN THE CORNER SHOP, DEIRDRE had secretly started developing feelings for Dev. Dev was over the moon with Deirdre's work on a stock report he'd asked her to do and expressed how grateful he was to her, flattering her with: 'Just remember, Deirdre, in your capable hands, the Alahan empire stands or falls.'

Deirdre then overheard Dev on the phone booking a restaurant table and assumed he was whisking her out for a posh meal to say thank you for her hard work. She rushed home in her lunch break to get changed – but her hopes of a romantic liaison with Dev were dashed when his new girlfriend Geena Gregory walked into the shop. Deirdre felt foolish when she realised that Dev hadn't booked the restaurant table for her, but it didn't stop her crush on Dev. She felt he offered her a rare bit of excitement in her life.

With her feelings for Dev growing, Deirdre started losing interest in Ken again at home. At Christmas, after a huge row with Ken and Peter, Deirdre stormed out – and straight into Dev's arms. All of Deirdre's pent-up passion for her shopkeeper boss Dev was released as they shared a one-night stand. But if Deirdre was hoping for a repeat performance, she would be disappointed. Dev didn't want anything to do with Deirdre after their night together, much to Deirdre's embarrassment.

2002

Ken's (almost) affair with Anita

GLASSES of 2002

KEN GAVE A TALK TO THE WEATHERFIELD HISTORICAL SOCIETY AT their meeting in Roy's Rolls. The chair of the society was Anita Scott, who took a fancy to Ken. Blanche noticed that Ken had an admirer in Anita and she told Deirdre to keep an eye on her rival.

Taking her mum's words on board, Deirdre tried to inject a bit of excitement into her relationship with Ken. She suggested a night out at the pictures but Ken told her he was too busy. She then went to the effort of cooking him a special dinner but when he arrived home Ken told her he'd already eaten, at Anita's house too. Deirdre was livid and wondered what Anita was up to with Ken. Worse was to come when Ken spent the night at Anita's house after she wined and dined him and got him too drunk to go home. Deirdre asked Blanche if she thought Ken was having a torrid affair but Blanche quickly reminded her: 'Well, I wouldn't call it torrid. It is Ken we're talking about.'

Ken saw Anita purely as a friend but Anita had other ideas. When she tried to kiss him, Ken backed off and told her that he wasn't interested. He told Deirdre all about Anita and Ken and Deirdre became close once again. They pulled together as a couple and realised just how deep their relationship was. Surely nothing could pull them apart from now on?

The beginning of the end of Mike and Ken's feud

KEN AND DEIRDRE HELD A SURPRISE PARTY FOR MIKE'S SIXTIETH birthday at No.1 and Mike was delighted when Adam turned up. The party signalled the beginning of the end of the feud between Mike and Ken.

Blanche started dating undertaker Archie Shuttleworth and brought him along to Mike's party. Archie's first words to Deirdre, after he looked her up and down to size her up, were: **'Five foot eight. I'm not wrong, am I?'**

As Mike's party was in full swing, Deirdre went into the backyard to have a cigarette. Dev followed her out and Deirdre laughed when he caught her smoking, saying Ken didn't like her smoking in the house. In the still night air with the sounds from the party gently escaping from the back door, Dev asked Deirdre why she had chosen Ken over dynamic, exciting Mike all those years ago.

'You don't love Ken,' Dev told her.

'Actually I do,' she replied. **'A lot more than I thought I did. Okay, so Ken might be in his sixties, he might not want to go out nightclubbing or wear expensive clothes, but he looks after me. He gets me through. And that's what it's all about, isn't it? Having somebody to go through it with.'**

Deirdre sighed heavily before carrying on and explaining her life to Dev. **'I was born one street away from here. I've lived in this street since I was twenty-one, went to school over there, my dad's buried about half a mile over there somewhere and that's probably where I'll finish up. This ... is my life ... right here ... having a cigarette in a poky little backyard while a houseful of people I've known most of my life eat sausage rolls and drink sherry. It might not be glamorous, but it's real and I like it.'**

Deirdre told Dev that since their passionate night at Christmas, she had opened her eyes to all that she had in her life. Their fling had made Deirdre realise all the

Blanche and her undertaker boyfriend, Archie Shuttleworth

Deirdre with Dev
in the corner shop

things she had been taking for granted, Ken included. Dev kissed her softly on the cheek, raised his glass to her and slowly walked away down the ginnel. Deirdre sighed and blew cigarette smoke into the dark night.

Deirdre gets the sack at the shop

AT THE CORNER SHOP, DEV ANNOUNCED TO DEIRDRE THAT HE WAS going to a sales conference and she asked if she could go with him. 'You?' he cried. **'You're the last person I'd want with me, after what happened at Christmas!'** His outburst was caught by girlfriend Geena, who wanted to know just what had happened at Christmas between Deirdre and Dev. He lied and told Geena that he'd had to let Deirdre down gently after she tried to kiss him under the mistletoe. However, Deirdre wasn't prepared to let Dev brush off their night of passion so lightly and she told Geena the truth about their one-night stand. Dev sacked Deirdre and she spent her days in Roy's Rolls, unable to tell Ken she'd lost her job, or the reason why. In the end, Deirdre and Dev made up and he re-employed her.

Tracy returns

TRACY RETURNED HOME TO WEATHERFIELD, HAVING LEFT HUSBAND Robert again. This time she was back for good. She lied to her mum that she'd found Robert in bed with her best friend, but it was Tracy who had been unfaithful.

Tracy landed at No. 1 right in the middle of Christmas dinner, when Deirdre was already struggling to cope with cooking for more people than she'd expected. Peter and Shelley Unwin were there and Sunita Parekh turned up. Blanche was supposed to be at Emily's but came back for Deirdre's dinner, jealous when Archie had turned up at Emily's with Audrey.

Deirdre realised she hadn't enough dinner to go round her extra guests and popped to Dev's corner shop for last-minute supplies. Dev was surprised and happy to see Deirdre and he mused that meeting at Christmas seemed to be becoming a tradition for them both. He was clearly after more than a kiss under the mistletoe from Deirdre but she cut him short and told him she wasn't interested this time. Knocked back by Deirdre, Dev's attention would soon wander to daughter Tracy instead.

Tracy's return
on Christmas Day

2003

Deirdre and Dev's secret exposed

WITH DEIRDRE'S ATTRACTIVE DAUGHTER TRACY BACK ON THE STREET, heads were turned and it wasn't long before Tracy caught Dev's eye. The two of them started sleeping together and Deirdre soon found out that her daughter and her ex-lover were a couple. Deirdre's eyes almost popped out of her head when she discovered Tracy and Dev were an item – she walked in on them snogging in the back room of the shop!

Deirdre discovers
Dev and Tracy are
an item

Ken decides to leave Deirdre after he finds out that she has slept with Dev

Deirdre tried to persuade Tracy to give up on Dev, but when Tracy demanded to know what her mum's problem was with her seeing Dev, Deirdre couldn't – and wouldn't – say. It was Dev's shop assistant Sunita who revealed the truth to Tracy. In the corner shop, Tracy had been boasting to Sunita that she wasn't like the rest of Dev's girls, saying she was special and different. Frustrated and fed up with Tracy, Sunita told her that she was exactly like the rest of Dev's girls; in fact, one of his girls was her mother!

Tracy was furious and went to Ken with the truth about Deirdre's sordid one-night stand with smoothie Dev. Ken was devastated. Just when it looked like he and Deirdre were back on track, he couldn't understand why she had done something like this.

When Blanche found out that Dev, the man Tracy was going out with, had slept with Deirdre too, she was horrified. However, she must have mellowed slightly in her old age because instead of slapping her wayward daughter, she hugged Deirdre and simply said: **'You stupid girl.'**

After Tracy had broken the news to Ken about Deirdre and Dev, Deirdre threw Tracy out of No.1. It was no surprise to any of them when Tracy moved in with Dev, although they wouldn't last long together. After Tracy moved out, Ken and Deirdre had some talking to do. Deirdre begged for Ken's forgiveness but in his anger, Ken flung horrendous insults at her.

It took a while, but Ken was finally able to forgive and forget and move on. Deirdre and Ken made up, yet again, with a joyous embrace.

GLASSES of 2003

Deirdre's a grandmother

WHEN TRACY ANNOUNCED SHE WAS PREGNANT, DEIRDRE WAS OVER-
joyed. She was going to be a grandmother at last! However, Deirdre would soon come
to wish that Tracy had never returned to their lives when the real news about the baby
was revealed.

Tracy was pregnant with Steve McDonald's baby but lied and claimed that Roy
Cropper was the father. Tracy had knocked Roy out with a date-rape drug and he
spent the night in her bed after Peter and Shelley's wedding. Tracy had slept with
Roy to win a one-penny bet she'd placed with Bev Unwin as a joke. When Deirdre
found out what Tracy had done, she spat out that she was ashamed to have her as
her daughter.

Worse was to come when Tracy blackmailed Roy and Hayley, demanding cash in
exchange for the baby. Tracy had so far kept everything secret from Deirdre and Ken
but Hayley thought it was about time they knew what their evil daughter was up to. In
a showdown in the Barlows' living room, Hayley told Deirdre and Ken about Tracy's
blackmail plan. There was a great deal of yelling and crying as Deirdre took the news
in and then looked at her daughter in disgust. She called Tracy a monster and an evil
little cow. **'That kidney was wasted on you!'** she spat.

Over the months to come and into the following year, Tracy caused ructions for
the Croppers and put them through hell. Tracy even went through with marrying

STREET SCENE

Roy, Hayley and
Patience Cropper

Roy Cropper. Roy thought that marrying Tracy would be the only way he would have any legal rights over the baby he wrongly thought was his. The situation become so fraught that Roy contemplated suicide and it was Hayley who found him, just in the nick of time, and saved his life. Tracy handed over her baby to Roy and Hayley in exchange for their money and the Croppers named her Patience. Despite everything she'd done and all the trouble she'd caused, Deirdre and Ken supported Tracy through her pregnancy. After all was said and done, Tracy was Deirdre's daughter, her baby would be her grandchild, and Deirdre defended her to the hilt.

It was at Steve McDonald's wedding to Karen when Tracy revealed that the baby's real dad was Steve. Roy and Hayley returned Patience Cropper to Tracy and she renamed her Amy Katherine Barlow.

ELSEWHERE IN 2003

Deirdre caught in the middle

Blanche and Archie the undertaker split up and it didn't take her long to move her attentions to wealthy Wally Bannister. When Tracy found out that her gran's new fella was worth a bob or two, she started wooing Wally herself and seduced him behind her gran's back. All was not as it seemed, however, when Wally turned out to be a gardener at the big posh house he said he lived in. He was married too.

Deirdre tracked Tracy down when she followed her to Wally's house and caught her daughter dallying with her mum's boyfriend. Wally explained that Deirdre had got it all wrong. **'Which bit have I got wrong?'** she yelled as she turned to Wally. **'You being a randy old beggar who's old enough to be her granddad?'** And then she turned to Tracy: **'Or you, being a gold-digging little tart?'** The row turned into a scuffle with both women ending up falling into the swimming pool.

Deirdre was disgusted with Tracy for going after Wally but they kept the news from Blanche. **'Listen, Tracy love,'** Deirdre said. **'She nearly had a heart attack when I told her Peter was a bigamist. If she found out that her boyfriend was cheating on her with her own granddaughter, it's liable to finish her off completely!'**

Working woman woes

In need of a new job after being sacked by Dev, Deirdre went for an interview at Mike's factory for the post of Assistant Manager. Experienced and mature Deirdre was interviewed alongside cheap and malleable Nick Tilsley. Deirdre was most put out when Mike offered the job to Nick.

Not wanting to let the grass grow under her feet, Deirdre then went for another interview at Weatherfield Town Hall. Last time she'd worked there was in her role as a councillor but this time she was taken on as a PA.

The return of Jon Lindsay?

When Deirdre's friend Bev Unwin told her she'd met a new bloke, Deirdre became very nervous indeed. Bev said her new fella was a dark-haired airline pilot called Jon. Deirdre had to make sure that Bev's new man wasn't the fake airline pilot and con man Jon Lindsay, so she spied on Bev and Jon in a bar when they were out on a date. Deirdre was relieved when Bev's new man wasn't the same Jon that she had once known. Bev couldn't understand why Deirdre was so obsessed with Jon and it was left to Mike to break the news to Bev about Deirdre's court case and prison sentence. Bev admired Deirdre for trying to protect her and the two of them became firm friends.

2004

Amy's christening

PROUD GRANDPARENTS DEIRDRE AND KEN ATTENDED THE CHRISTENING of their granddaughter, Amy. Despite the evil, nasty way Tracy had behaved towards Roy and Hayley throughout her pregnancy, Deirdre supported her. Ken always saw straight through Tracy's viciousness and refused to get involved but Deirdre stood firm with Ken over the baby: **'I'm going to help her. And you ought to help her too, Ken, because this is our grandchild we're talking about!'** It wasn't the first time, and it certainly wouldn't be the last time, that Deirdre would support Tracy, however evil her actions would become.

Deirdre feels the force of Blanche's acid tongue

AT DEV AND SUNITA'S ENGAGEMENT PARTY IN THE ROVERS, BLANCHE turned her acid tongue onto Deirdre. **'And don't think I've not seen you,'** Blanche remarked out of nowhere.

Deirdre rowing with
Blanche in the Rovers

'What?' replied Deirdre, surprised.

'**Looking at Dev with that look, all wistful. You had your chance and you chose Ken over all them shops. Not one of the wisest moves.**'

Deirdre was shocked. '**Are you saying that I should have dumped Ken for Dev?**'

'**You've married foreign once,**' Blanche replied. '**You could have done it again … and got a shop out of it in a divorce settlement! You could have then got back together with Ken but with a bit of capital under your stocking top.**'

Deirdre shook her head in disbelief. '**Well, for your information, Dev didn't want me. Not that I'd have chosen him over Ken anyway.**'

'**You know what you've done?**' Blanche asked Deirdre, before telling her in no uncertain terms. '**You've settled. All your life you've settled for second best. You're a big disappointment to me, Deirdre.**'

Fortunately, Blanche had the heart to apologise to Deirdre later.

Mike and Deirdre share a secret moment

AWAY FROM HER MUM AT DEV'S ENGAGEMENT PARTY IN THE PUB, Deirdre and Mike had a candid chat. He started by jokingly asking her if she was jealous that Dev was getting engaged to someone other than her.

'For your information,' Deirdre told Mike, '**Ken has proposed to me. On more than one occasion, actually.**'

'So why haven't you tied the knot?' Mike asked. 'Are you waiting for a better offer?'

'No!' she said. '**Although I wouldn't expect you to believe that.**'

There was a misty look in Mike's eye as he said: '**Let me tell you something. I should never have let you go. That time you decided to stay with Ken I shouldn't have given up on you. We could have saved ourselves a lot of bother. I could have been a good husband to you.**'

'**For a while, till something younger caught your eye,**' said Deirdre. '**Thanks very much, Mike, but I chose the better man. I think we both know that.**'

Deirdre plays the harmonica

DEIRDRE PROVED SHE WAS A WOMAN OF MANY TALENTS WHEN SHE GOT a tune out of a harmonica in the bar at the Rovers! Sean Tully had just arrived on Coronation Street and was in need of a place to stay. Blanche gave him the name of a good B&B and in searching through his pockets to find a pen to write its name down, he pulled out a harmonica.

'**Oh! I used to have one of these, do you remember?**' Deirdre squealed to Blanche in delight.

'**I keep catching my lip,**' moaned Sean.

'**Oh, you're not doing it right,**' Deirdre told him. She picked up the harmonica and expertly played a lively rendition of the old minstrel song 'Oh! Susanna'. Everyone in the pub clapped along in delight. She later played a second tune on the mouth organ, a mournful version of 'Amazing Grace'.

THE REAL WORLD
IN 2004

Greece host the
Olympics in Athens

Cockle pickers die
at Morecambe Bay

Louis Armstrong dies

Eurodisney opens

Deirdre flirting
with Charlie Stubbs
in the pub

Deirdre works as PA at the council

ON DEIRDRE'S FIRST DAY AT HER NEW JOB AT THE COUNCIL, KEN cooked lamb chops as a surprise dinner for her. But Deirdre didn't come straight home from work and Ken was angry when he found her drinking in the Rovers and flirting with builder Charlie Stubbs. Deirdre followed Ken home and ate her burnt lamb chops while Ken told her not to trust Charlie, especially as he'd seen asbestos in his builder's yard. Deirdre said she would have a word with someone at the council about it, but all she did was ask Charlie to move it, which he did. He kept on Deirdre's good side and assumed she had some influence over choosing which building firms received the lucrative contracts from the council.

When Charlie's firm was given the council contract for the windows at Bessie Street School, he showed his appreciation to Deirdre by buying her some flowers. Bev saw the bouquet and jealously assumed the two of them were having an affair. She told Ken her suspicions and Ken and Deirdre sat down to have a chat, a familiar one to both of them by now. This time it was Deirdre who denied she was playing away from home.

Barlows in TV quiz show

BLANCHE ENTERED THE BARLOWS TO TAKE PART IN A TV GAME SHOW called *Top of the Tree*. The Barlows needed seven people in their team to qualify to take part so along with Ken, Deirdre, Blanche, Tracy and Amy (who answered a question correctly, about *Teletubbies*), they roped in Liz and Steve too.

STREET PEOPLE

Liz McDonald
and son Steve

The pressure was on as the team did well and then Steve was put in the spotlight to win a car and a large cash prize if he could answer a question about shoes. He was allowed one phone call and rang wife Karen, who had no idea where Steve was or why he was asking her about shoes. If Steve had told Karen he was on a quiz show being filmed in London with Tracy, Karen's arch-rival for Steve's affections, Karen would have gone mad. Karen answered Steve's question correctly and Team Barlow won the top prize of a new car.

When Steve arrived back in Weatherfield, Blanche spilled the beans to Karen about the London trip. Karen was furious with Steve and demanded the prize car she had won.

Deirdre begs Mike to drop charges against Tracy

Deirdre pleads with Mike

TRACY ENDED UP IN TROUBLE AFTER SHE HAD A FLING WITH CIARAN McCarthy. With the help of Mike's girlfriend, Penny King, Ciaran invested £5,000 in a restaurant. However, he was forced to sell it when the venture didn't take off. Tracy told Ciaran to lie to Penny about losing her investment but he told Penny the truth. When Mike found out about Tracy's scam, he wanted to turn her in to the police.

Determined to save her daughter from going to prison, Deirdre got down on her knees to beg Mike not to turn Tracy in.

ELSEWHERE IN 2004

Edie and Jack as Ida Fagg in the ladies bowling competition.

Deirdre joined the Rovers' Ravers – the pub's ladies' bowling team – when they battled against the team from the Slaughterman's Arms. When the team was one lady short to make up the full quota, Jack Duckworth dressed up in drag as team member Ida Fagg.

Deirdre was celebrated in poetry when Ken penned an ode to her in the Most Romantic Couple competition at the Rovers. She was delighted when Ken's love poem won second prize. First prize was won by Claire Casey and Ashley Peacock when Ashley got down on one knee and proposed.

2005

Deirdre finally accepts Ken's proposal

Deirdre and Ken,
happy again

KEN PROPOSED TO DEIRDRE AGAIN, TELLING HER THAT MARRIAGE would suit them both for all kinds of reasons, not least benefit entitlement, pension and tax. Deirdre turned him down as it was obvious Ken hadn't proposed for romantic reasons. Being rejected again by Deirdre, Ken drowned his sorrows in the Rovers when Fred gave him some advice: '**A woman wants a bouquet, not a balance sheet.**' Tracy also did her best to make Ken see sense and after a night in the Rovers, he decided to propose again. As Deirdre and Ken walked back home from the pub one rainy night, Ken stopped Deirdre by the front door of No.1 before she could go inside.

'**Deirdre, I love you,**' he said. '**You must know that, surely?**'

'Course I do, and I love you,' she replied.

'**So?**' Ken said. '**Look ... come here,**' and he led Deirdre by the hand to Maxine Peacock's bench outside of the hair salon.

'**Now, this time I'm going to do it properly,**' he said.

'**Don't be silly, it's raining!**' laughed Deirdre.

'**Sit down, sit down,**' implored Ken.

Deirdre sat on Maxine's bench and Ken got down on one knee in front of her.

'**Oh, you're joking!**' Deirdre laughed when she realised what Ken was doing.

'**Deirdre,**' he said in all seriousness. '**Deirdre, you know I love you and want to spend the rest of my life caring for you. Will you make me the happiest man in the world by becoming my wife?**'

Deirdre laughed and kissed Ken. '**Yes!**' she cried. '**Of course I will!**'

Their wedding date was set and it was all systems go for the remarriage of Ken and Deirdre ... until Ray Langton returned to her life after twenty-seven years.

Ken proposes
to Deirdre
on Maxine's bench

Deirdre reunited with Ray Langton

DEIRDRE'S FIRST HUSBAND RAY LANGTON shocked everyone when he returned to the Street for the first time since leaving for the Netherlands in 1978. It was on the morning of Deirdre and Ken's wedding day that he drove his car onto the cobbles. As he drove down the street and looked around his old haunt, his car gently bumped into Amy's pushchair and Tracy went ballistic. She had no idea the driver of the car was her dad, having had nothing to do with him since he left her as a baby. The jolt to Amy's pushchair made the baby cry and Tracy overreacted, yelling at Ray: '**You could have killed her!**'

She rushed Amy to A&E and Ray, feeling guilty for causing the woman so much anguish, followed her to the hospital to ensure her child was okay. At the hospital, Tracy told Ray that the accident had caused her to miss her parents' wedding.

Ken and Deirdre braced themselves to enter the register office to repeat their vows just as Tracy rang them to tell them about the car accident. The wedding was called off and everyone trooped to the hospital, concerned for Amy's welfare.

When she walked into the hospital, Deirdre received the shock of her life, coming face to face with Ray. She introduced Ray to Tracy as her dad and the shock of it all was too much for Ray: he suffered a collapse in the hospital foyer. Ray stayed on in

Weatherfield to recover and Emily took him in at her house. He and Deirdre shared a tender moment as he revealed the real reason for his return was that he was terminally ill with stomach cancer.

'**So come on, why are you here?**' she asked.

'**To make up for lost time.**'

'**With Tracy?**'

Ray nodded. '**Mostly. And with Amy, now I know about her.**'

Deirdre said: '**You'll have your work cut out. As far as Tracy's concerned you might as well be dead.**'

'**Do you think she'll let me make it up to her?**' he asked.

'**I wouldn't hold your breath. She can be very stubborn and she likes nothing more than holding a grudge.**'

'**That's a pity,**' Ray said. '**I haven't got much time.**'

'**What? And then you're going back?**' Deirdre asked.

'**And then I'm going to die,**' he replied.

Ken worried that Deirdre might have unfinished romantic business with Ray. He quickly rebooked the register office for 8 April so that Deirdre wouldn't have time to change her mind about marrying him.

The Hen
at her hen party

Deirdre's hen night

Deirdre, Tracy, Liz,
Rita, Emily, Eileen
and Sunita at
Deirdre's hen party
in the Rovers

AS HER WEDDING DAY TO KEN APPROACHED, DEIRDRE WAS TAKEN OUT on her hen night with just the right amount of friends to each wear one of the letters from her name on a T-shirt. These were: Tracy (D), Frankie Baldwin (E), Liz (I), Eileen Grimshaw (R), Emily (D), Rita (R) and Sunita (E). However, poorly Ray didn't see the funny side when Tracy (D), Liz (I) and Frankie (E) stood in front of him in their T-shirts as the girls got ready for their big night out.

Deirdre wore pink angel wings and devil horns and the hens went out for pizza and cheap wine in town. On his stag do in the Rovers, Ken sat with Ray, Mike and Dev – men who had woken up with Deirdre by their side in the past. Ken proposed a toast to himself, saying he was the luckiest man in the world.

THE REAL WORLD
IN 2005
....
The Labour
government wins
a third term
....
Fox hunting banned
....
Licensing laws
relaxed
....
Ellen MacArthur
sails solo around
the world
....
David Cameron
chosen as leader of
the Conservatives

⟨ 147 ⟩

Deirdre and Ken remarry

KEN AND DEIRDRE REMARRIED AT WEATHERFIELD REGISTER OFFICE ON 8 April 2005. Ken's grandson Adam was best man and local butcher Fred Elliott took the wedding photos – **'Everyone say sausages!'**

At their wedding reception in the Rovers, Ray congratulated the happy couple and even Mike gave them both his best wishes. Emily looked on as Ken kissed his bride. **'If ever a couple were meant for each other ...'** she started to say before Blanche jumped in with **'... until one of probably be my daughter! He's sixty-five, she's not turned fifty yet and she's been making a fool of herself since her twenties.'**

Tracy shared a dance with her dad and apologised to him for being so awful when he'd returned to the Street.

them messes it up again, and it'll

After the dance, Ray sat down in the pub, clutched his chest in pain and let out a groan. Blanche went to sit beside Ray and had a quiet word with her ex-son-in-law: **'You know I've never liked you, Ray. But I'm glad that you've finally faced your responsibilities and made your peace with Tracy. You're not such a bad 'un after all.'** But it was too late. Ray had not heard Blanche's words; he had passed away as she spoke. Tracy was hysterical: **'Not now, not yet. Ray! Dad!'**

Determined not to let anything spoil Ken and Deirdre's honeymoon, Tracy offered to make all of Ray's funeral arrangements and sent her mum and Ken off on honeymoon. Deirdre left with tears in her eyes.

Deirdre tries to give up smoking

WHEN KEN AND DEIRDRE RETURNED FROM HONEYMOON, DEIRDRE TRIED to stop smoking, as a wedding present to Ken – and herself.

'I've got a nicotine patch on this arm and a HRT patch on the other,' she moaned.

Ken even instructed Norris not to sell cigs to Deirdre from the Kabin. In retaliation, Deirdre told Ken he had to give up his coffee habit of fifteen cups a day. While Deirdre tried to stay off the fags, Ken caved in and went back on the coffee. The two of them were as bad-tempered with each other in a way that only two people trying to give up lifelong addictions could be.

Their behaviour had not gone unnoticed by Blanche. 'When it comes to gay badinage, you make your Uncle Albert look like Liberace!' she told Ken.

E L S E W H E R E   I N   2 0 0 5

Deirdre celebrated her fiftieth birthday but was more than a little disappointed when there was no surprise party. 'But you told me not to arrange anything!' an exasperated Ken told her. Deirdre rolled her eyes at him. Would he never learn?

Deirdre supported her friend Bev when her daughter Shelley suffered domestic abuse at the hands of builder Charlie Stubbs. After Shelley saw sense and jilted Charlie at the altar, Deirdre was horrified when Tracy started dating Charlie. Deirdre tried to warn her daughter off but Tracy wouldn't listen. Tracy and Charlie's relationship would go on to have deadly consequences, bringing murder and mayhem to Deirdre's door.

STREET PEOPLE

Charlie Stubbs

2006

Mike Baldwin dies in Ken's arms

WHEN DEIRDRE HEARD THAT MIKE HAD BEEN DIAGNOSED WITH Alzheimer's disease, she called at his flat to see him. She found Mike sitting on the living-room floor, looking through old photos and listening to music. It broke Deirdre's heart to see Mike in that state. With a bit of effort she put on a smile and sat next to him on the floor …

F R O M   S C R I P T   T O   S C R E E N :

CORONATION STREET   EP#6254   TX:22/03/2006

DEIRDRE
(softly)
Mike?

MIKE
(as if they'd never been apart)
Oh, hello, love. When did you get in? You want a Scotch?

DEIRDRE
I shouldn't. Ken'll think you've been getting me tiddly.

MIKE
What's Barlow coming round for?

DEIRDRE
He's not. Doesn't matter. Go on, just a small one.

MIKE
(affectionately)
It's not been all bad, has it, Deirdre? Me and you?

DEIRDRE
Course not.

MIKE
When I shake off this cold we'll go to Spain for a couple of weeks, eh? Just you and me. How's that sound?

SHE BLINKS BACK HER TEARS, MANAGES ANOTHER SMILE. SHE GENTLY STROKES MIKE'S FACE.

DEIRDRE
Yeah. Be lovely.

MUSIC FILTERS AROUND THE ROOM.

MIKE
Dance with me
(standing and taking Deirdre's hand)
Come on - you were always a great little mover.

DEIRDRE STANDS, CLOSE TO TEARS. MIKE HOLDS HER TIGHTLY AS THEY DANCE TO DUSTY SPRINGFIELD.

MIKE
This is nice, isn't it?

DEIRDRE CHOKES BACK THE TEARS AND KISSES MIKE GENTLY ON THE HEAD.

Days later, with Mike wearing nothing but his pyjamas, dressing gown and slippers, he shuffled through the Weatherfield streets in the cold night air. He was seriously ill, scared and confused, and had no idea where he was going.

As Ken left the Rovers to walk back home, he saw Mike standing on the cobbles, looking at the factory ...

CORONATION STREET   EP#6265   TX:07/04/2006

KEN
(shocked)
Mike?

MIKE TURNS, WRETCHED AND DISHEVELLED. WHEN HE SEES KEN HIS FACE BRIGHTENS.

MIKE
Barlow ...

KEN RUSHES TO MIKE'S SIDE.

KEN
What are you doing here? Look at the state of you!

MIKE
Factory's closed ...

KEN
Let's get you inside ...

MIKE MOVES FURTHER TOWARDS THE FACTORY DOOR.

MIKE
I haven't got my keys ...

KEN
I'll take you to mine ... get you warm ... here ...

KEN TAKES HIS JACKET OFF AND PUT IT AROUND MIKE'S SHOULDERS.

KEN
You're meant to be in hospital.

MIKE
I always put my keys in my pocket.

KEN
(gently)
Mike, you're in your pyjamas.

SUDDENLY, MIKE FALLS. KEN GOES DOWN WITH HIM, CATCHING HIM AS HE LANDS HEAVILY ON THE FACTORY STEPS.

KEN
(takes out his phone)
Ambulance ... Yes, hello, I need an ambulance ... Baldwin, Mike Baldwin ... he doesn't look at all well, please hurry.

MIKE
(staring at Ken)
What are you doing here, Barlow?

KEN
Looking after you.

MIKE
I don't need looking after. Where's Deirdre?

KEN
She's at work. She'll be home soon.

MIKE
Yeah ... but whose home? You should know, about me and Deirdre ...

KEN
I know.

MIKE
(seeming surprised)
She told you?

KEN
Mike, that was a long time ago.

MIKE
No, no, she's gonna leave you, bring the kid, Tracy, bring her and live with me. You're finished, Barlow ... Deirdre loves me ... She's mine ...
(Mike's whole body tenses as a massive heart attack surges through him)

KEN
(explodes)
Mike! Mike! No! ... No, you don't, Baldwin ... No! Come on, Baldwin!

Mike's body slumped backwards against Ken as the life drained from him.

Ken couldn't move. The man who had for so much of Ken's life been his sworn enemy was now lying dead in his arms.

When Blanche found out that Mike had passed away she was less than sympathetic. She had only one thing to say: '**I bet Deirdre's glad she picked Ken now!**'

Deirdre and Ken
at Mike's funeral

Mike's will leaves
the factory to Adam

Deirdre kisses the council man

GLASSES of 2006

ON A DRUNKEN NIGHT OUT WITH THE GIRLS IN THE WEATHERFIELD Arms, Deirdre ended up snogging a stranger at the bar.

The man turned out to be waiting on a planning decision at Weatherfield Council, where Deirdre worked. He blackmailed Deirdre and told her he'd tell Ken about their passionate kiss if she didn't do him a favour by processing his application. Eileen advised Deirdre not to do it: **'Two dafts don't make a sensible!'** But Deirdre did as the man asked, and bumped up his planning application to the top of the pile.

Eccles arrives

BLANCHE WENT TO THE FUNERAL OF HER FRIEND LENA THISTLEWOOD. She kept the pledge she'd made to Lena before she died that she would dress in a scarlet suit for her funeral in a two-fingered salute to the Grim Reaper. After the funeral, Blanche returned with Lena's little dog, a Border terrier called Lady Freckles.

Lena had left the dog to Blanche in her will. Amy couldn't pronounce the dog's name properly and so the Barlows changed it to Eccles. Deirdre and the dog got on like old pals and she took it with her for company on her ciggie breaks in the backyard.

THE REAL WORLD
IN 2006

Last edition of
Top of the Pops

Italy wins the World
Cup in Germany

Charles Darwin's
tortoise dies at
the age of 176

Sunita's hen night in the back room of the Rovers

Liz's hen night in the Rovers

Deirdre's
FRIENDS

One of the girls

DEIRDRE WAS ALWAYS AT THE HEART OF ANY EVENT GOING ON IN *Coronation Street*. She was one of the girls, always up for a good night out and in the thick of it whenever she could.

Deirdre, Eileen and Liz formed a friendship, supporting each other and offering a shoulder to lean on, usually after they'd shared a glass or two of wine. Whether they were moaning about their men or wailing over their wayward offspring, the three women were there for each other. Girls' nights out were more often than not held in the Rovers, with caterwauling through karaoke usually involved.

Karaoke queens – Liz, Deirdre and Eileen

Deirdre and Emily watch as Blanche takes to the Street in her mobility scooter

Deirdre and Blanche celebrate with Emily and Ken on their birthday, 2009

Emily Bishop

EMILY WAS DEIRDRE'S OLDEST AND MOST trusted friend. She became godmother to Deirdre's daughter Tracy and took them both in to live with her when they had nowhere to go.

Deirdre and Eileen
on the red wine

Deirdre sums up her life to Eileen

DEIRDRE AND EILEEN ONCE GOT A LITTLE TIPSY ON RED WINE AND asked the really important questions about life ...

Deirdre: 'Do you know, when I die and I get to the pearly gates and thingummy asks me to sum my life up in one word, I shall just say, "Disappointed"...'

Eileen: 'With an undercurrent of fear. Disappointed with an undercurrent of fear.'

Deirdre: 'Aw . . . what are you frightened of?'

Eileen: 'Life's frightening at the best of times and there's always some problem that comes and slaps you round the face. Anyway, let's just get hammered and forget all about it.'

Deirdre: 'Tell me about it. You should try walking in my shoes.'

Eileen: 'Are they not comfy?'

Deirdre walked downstairs at Eileen's house, singing along to Rihanna ...'I like your potpourri in the bathroom,' she told Eileen. 'You don't see much potpourri these days. Don't worry, I didn't eat it.'

A friend to the last

WHEN DEIRDRE'S CLOSE FRIEND BEV UNVIN LEFT WEATHERFIELD AFTER Fred Elliott died, they kept in touch. Deirdre went to stay with Bev when she was poorly in 2010. Deirdre visited Bev again in 2011 and 2012.

When Deirdre left in 2014 to escape the pressures of Peter's trial for the murder of Tina McIntyre, she went to stay with Bev. Ken spent Christmas with Deirdre at Bev's and stayed on longer than expected when Bev's brother died. It was at Bev's house that Deirdre passed away in the summer of 2015. Bev had to give the heartbreaking news to her family.

Deirdre at Bev Unwin's wedding day to Fred Elliott. Fred died before he got to the church

Deirdre comforts Bev at the police station when she reports Charlie Stubbs to the cops

Deirdre punched **Tricia Hopkins** after she spread false rumours about Ray having an affair

Maggie Redman revealed Deirdre's affair with Mike Baldwin to Tracy

Deirdre's
FOES

Denise Osbourne was the mother of Ken's son Daniel. Deirdre slapped her in the Rovers

Ken's affair with **Wendy Crozier** would split the Barlow marriage apart

Deirdre walked in on **Sue Jeffers** and Ken in bed together at No. 1

Deirdre and Tracy
shared some ugly
home truths in this
two-hander episode

2007

Deirdre and Tracy star in two-hander

IN *CORONATION STREET*'S ENTIRE HISTORY OF THOUSANDS OF EPI-
sodes, there have been only two episodes featuring just two characters. In January
2000, Curly and Raquel Watts were reunited in a millennium special. And in 2007
there was a tense two-hander when Tracy Barlow confessed to Deirdre that she'd
killed Charlie Stubbs.

Charlie Stubbs was a nasty piece of work. He was a manipulative, abusive woman-
iser and his relationship with Tracy was twisted and violent. Tracy gave as good as she
got from Charlie, proving she could be as dangerous as him. As each of them pressed
the other's buttons, their relationship became savage and brutal. Tracy lied and said
she was pregnant so that Charlie would give her money to have an abortion. It was
money she spent on a new pair of shoes. When Charlie found out he warned her never
to cross him again, and destroyed one of the expensive shoes she had bought. He even
beat up Tracy's stepbrother Peter. Charlie also slept with ex-girlfriend Shelley and she
ended up pregnant with his child. Still Tracy didn't dump him. **'You've got no self-
respect!'** Deirdre yelled at her daughter.

It was when Tracy found out that Charlie was having an affair with Maria Sutherland
that she decided to exact her revenge. Tracy managed to convince her family
and friends that Charlie was physically abusing her. She went as far as deliberately

burning her arm with the iron and then told everyone that Charlie had done it.

Tracy then lured Charlie into a false sense of security one night at home. As he sat on the sofa, Tracy danced a sexy dance in front of him, wearing a miniskirt, tight top and heels. Charlie was loving it, lost in the moment, and then Tracy whacked him over the head with a heavy ornament. The blow to the head killed Charlie, and Tracy was charged with his murder.

Deirdre destroys the video tape

DAVID PLATT BLACKMAILED TRACY, SAYING HE WOULDN'T TESTIFY IN her defence unless she slept with him. In an effort to keep David on her side, she snogged him outside of Charlie Stubbs's flat – but their kiss was caught on CCTV. Deirdre found out about the taped kiss from Jason Grimshaw, who handed Deirdre the video to watch at home. Still believing that Tracy was innocent of killing Charlie, Deirdre destroyed the tape.

Deirdre do
best to stop
attacking S
Unwin aft
found out s
pregnant
Charlie's

Deirdre is horrified
when Tracy claims
she's killed Charlie in
self-defence

Tracy confesses to murder

TRACY PLEADED SELF-DEFENCE, BUT IN THE TWO-HANDER EPISODE SET on the eve of Tracy's court trial, she confessed Charlie's murder to Deirdre. Over a bottle of red wine, Deirdre reminded Tracy how much she meant to her. '**If I didn't love you, Tracy, I'd be up them stairs. Dreaming of me and Rod Stewart running through the surf. But I'm not, am I? I'm down here with you. Going out of my mind.**'

Since Charlie's death, Deirdre had suffered panic attacks. She told Tracy she wasn't prepared to stand up in court and defend her, because she knew, deep in her heart, that Tracy's self-defence plea was a lie. Tracy was incensed, accused Deirdre of turning her back on her and screamed at Deirdre across the dining-room table:

'**Most mothers would take the stand and stand up for their daughters!**'

'**And most daughters wouldn't have murdered their boyfriends!**' Deirdre yelled back.

'**He wasn't just any old boyfriend, you vicious cow!**' Tracy spat.

'Oh, I'm not saying he didn't deserve to die,' Deirdre said.

'**So what are you having a go at me for, then?**'

'**Because I want you to be honest with me!**' Deirdre yelled. '**Every word that comes out of your mouth, Tracy, I just don't trust it because your eyes tell a different story. I know you, Tracy. I know you better than anyone in the whole world. I carried you for nine months and I know ... I know that there is some-thing seriously wrong here. And I want you to tell me what it is. Tracy, whatever it is, I'll understand. I'll try.**'

Deirdre laid into Tracy, bringing up all her wrongdoings – date-raping Roy Cropper; selling Amy to Roy and Hayley; taking ecstasy and finishing up on a life-support machine. Spent, Deirdre started to cry, all of her pent-up emotion spilling out as she blamed Tracy for the death of her Moroccan husband: '**You messed up your body and my Samir died as a result! The one man I—**' but Tracy cut her short before she could finish.

'**The one man ... what? The one man you loved? I can't believe you're saying that Samir was the love of your life.**'

'I felt fat, I felt frumpy, I felt forty,' Deirdre said. '**And he tells me I'm gorgeous and interesting and alive. Why shouldn't I have him on a pedestal? Don't you dare be flippant about him, when you're walking around with his kidney inside you. It's the only decent thing about you!**'

Tracy circled Deirdre and then went for the kill ...

'Fag-ash Lil with a glass of Merlot in her hand. Why d'you think I got into drugs in the first place? To get away from you and your glasses and your necklines and your moaning and your coughing and everything always stinking of fags! I remember you, I remember your tacky perm and your loose morals. "Oi, Tracy Barlow, your mam's a slag!" That's what they used to say to me at school. I didn't know who was going to wake up in your bed next.'

GLASSES of 2007

Deirdre slaps Tracy

Deirdre slapped Tracy hard across the face and ran out the back door into the ginnel for a cigarette. Tracy followed her and tried to apologise: '**Your perm wasn't that bad,**' she said. '**It was the eighties!**'

'**I don't hate you, Tracy,**' Deirdre cried. '**I don't like you very much sometimes, but it's not hate. And the love is unfaltering. I'd lie for you, you know. But in order to do that I need to know what I'm lying about. I want to know what really happened.**'

'**And then you'd go on the stand?**' Tracy asked, getting her hopes raised. She knew that if she told Deirdre the truth she might just convince her mum to lie in court to save her.

Deirdre did take the witness box at Tracy's trial and lied through her teeth but it did nothing to help. Deirdre was devastated when the court found Tracy guilty of murder. As Tracy was sentenced to fifteen years in HMP Norcross, Deirdre's wail of '**Tracy, love!**' echoed around the courtroom.

However, Tracy would be released three years later when the forensics expert who gave evidence at her trial was exposed as a fraud.

THE REAL WORLD
IN 2007

Smoking in public
places banned

HM the Queen
becomes the oldest
British monarch

The *Cutty Sark*
burns

Britain's Got Talent
launches

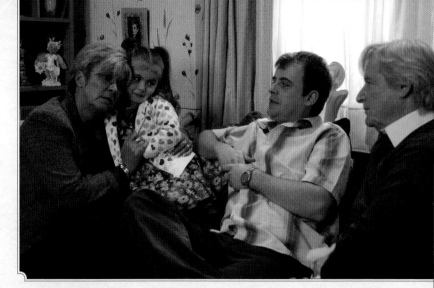

Deirdre, Amy, Steve
and Ken contemplate
life without Tracy

Deirdre and Ken split up – again

TO COPE WITH THE STRAIN OF HAVING A MURDERER FOR A DAUGHTER,
Deirdre made a new house rule and started smoking indoors, much to Ken's annoyance. When he protested, Deirdre told him: **'Sometimes you sound just like that
bloke with the pointy ears from *Star Trek*!'**

Ken and Deirdre's marriage started to crumble as they struggled to cope with
Tracy being locked up. Ken threatened to leave but Blanche thought he wouldn't:
'You're all gong and no dinner,' she said. But Ken called her bluff, packed his bags
and walked out of No.1 to stay in a B&B.

The guest house Ken stayed in was close to the hair salon where his ex-lover
Denise was now working, and he called in to see her one day. He asked if she was free
for a quick chat. **'You want five minutes when you've not seen us for ten years?'**
Denise asked him, shocked to find Ken had turned up out of the blue.

Ken and Deirdre's
relationship under
strain again

Ken gets caught in the crossfire between Deirdre and Denise in the Rovers

Blanche wondered what Ken was up to at the B&B and she followed him one day as he went to see Denise. She gave the news to Deirdre, who stormed round to Denise's flat to find out what he was doing there. Denise had offered nothing more to Ken than a night on her sofa and a chance to spend some time with his son Daniel, but Deirdre believed there was more going on. It was left to Denise to have a word with Ken, telling him to go home. Ken knew Deirdre wouldn't take his word for it that there was nothing between him and Denise, and he asked Denise to go with him as backup.

But when Denise and Ken walked into the Rovers to talk to Deirdre, the insults started and then fists flew. In the fracas that followed, Denise called Deirdre a '**scrawny-faced fishwife**'. Deirdre stung back with '**You slapper!**' and hit Denise hard across the face. This led to Ken calling Deirdre '**a deranged harpie**' while Blanche looked on, tutting and rolling her eyes.

Deirdre and Ken reunite

IN LIFE THERE ARE SOME THINGS THAT SHOULD ALWAYS COME IN pairs, like socks and Barlows. And it didn't take long before Deirdre and Ken were back together again. When Deirdre returned home after a night out in town with the girls, she found Ken waiting for her with a huge bouquet. They shared a hug and some tears before he whisked her upstairs for a cuddle. Blanche went outside, looked to the sky and whispered, '**Thank you.**'

STREET SCENE

Liz McDonald's wedding day to Vernon Tomlin

ELSEWHERE IN 2007

Deirdre was caught in the thick of it on Liz McDonald and Vernon Tomlin's wedding day. After a punch-up between Vernon and Liz's ex-husband Jim, Deirdre had to stand up in front of the guests to announce that the wedding had been cancelled. '**Betty'll not be best pleased,**' said Rita. '**She's got two hundred and fifty vol-au-vents waiting!**' As the wedding guests trooped out of the register office, Steve arrived with news that his mum's wedding was back on. '**Could you all go back inside!**' Deirdre yelled to the crowd before taking her place by Liz's side as her witness.

Ken comes in to find
Deirdre reading his
manuscript. He's
furious with her and
tells her she's been
holding him back
all his life. In reply,
Deirdre slaps him!

2008

Ken burns his book

KEN STARTED EDITING HIS NOVEL THAT HE'D WRITTEN MANY YEARS ago. The book was about a man who felt he had wasted his life when he married a woman far beneath him. He called the book *Sunday Afternoon*, which prompted Blanche to tell Deirdre: **'You were conceived on a Sunday afternoon!'**

Although Ken swore it wasn't autobiographical, Deirdre was annoyed by the book's implications. It led to another argument between them. In the heat of their fight, Ken admitted that, yes, he was disappointed with his life, their house, and even with Deirdre! In her fury, she slapped Ken hard across the face before storming off to Eileen's for a glass of wine. While Deirdre was out, Ken decided to burn the book in the backyard and by the time Deirdre returned home, Ken's literary creation was cremated.

Fancy a Deirdre?

AFTER THEIR ARGUMENT, DEIRDRE MADE UP WITH KEN IN THE LIVING room of No.1. They shared a cuddle by Uncle Albert's framed photograph and then Ken propositioned his wife.

'Do you fancy having a Deirdre in the backyard?' he asked her.

'You what?' replied Deirdre in surprise.

Ken explained that he'd overheard the locals in the pub asking to 'have a Deirdre' at the bar. It meant to drink wine from really big glasses. Cheers!

THE REAL WORLD
IN 2008

China hosts the
Olympics in Beijing

*Batman: The Dark
Knight* released

UK experiences
largest earthquake
(5.2) in 25 years

Prince Harry
returns to the UK
from Afghanistan

Peter kisses Leanne as Simon comes out of his room — Leanne makes her excuses and leaves

Deirdre's second grandchild

PETER BARLOW RETURNED WITH HIS SON SIMON AFTER SIMON'S MUM, Lucy, died. Parental responsibility was thrust on a reluctant and inexperienced Peter. Ken and Deirdre took Peter and Simon in at No.1 and supported Peter as he struggled to learn to be a dad. They were overjoyed to have their grandson living with them. It took Simon a while to settle in and open up, and he was so quiet when he first arrived that Blanche named him Shymon.

The One O'clock Club

WHEN BLANCHE ANNOUNCED SHE WAS OFF ON A PILGRIMAGE TO Lourdes with the One O'Clock Club, she asked Deirdre to accompany her. Deirdre agreed to keep her mum company, only to discover that Blanche had put her name down as an unpaid carer to look after the old folks on the trip. Deirdre even ended up going alone when Blanche upset fellow club members who banned her from the trip.

Carla's hen night

BEFORE CARLA CONNOR'S WEDDING TO TONY GORDON, DEIRDRE joined in the fun at the Rovers on Carla's hen night. When the male stripper arrived, the girls went wild. Liz sprayed his chest with squirty cream. **'Hey!'** Deirdre screamed. **'Ken likes that cream, we have it on our apple crumble!'**

Even though it was her big night, Carla wasn't in the mood for celebrating. She knew she didn't love Tony, it was Liam Connor her heart was set on. Deirdre found Carla standing outside the pub in the cold night air and Carla asked if she could have one of Deirdre's cigarettes.

'I didn't know you smoked,' Deirdre told her.

'It's been thirteen years since I had one.'

'Are you nervous?' Deirdre asked.

'Just sifting through old memories,' Carla replied.

'Well, I'll smoke to them!' Deirdre laughed.

Deirdre asked Carla why she was so upset and wondered if she'd made the right decision to be wed. Carla started crying.

'It's nothing that a bit of lippy won't sort out,' she told Deirdre.

'It'd be lippy and a time machine in my case,' Deirdre laughed. **'Nothing that a bit of lippy won't sort out … now there's a rule to live your life by!'**

GLASSES of 2008

2009

No plain sailing for Deirdre and Ken

WOULD DEIRDRE AND KEN'S MARRIAGE EVER BE SMOOTH SAILING? IT would seem not, when Ken found himself torn between a new life and the one he had shared for so long with Deirdre.

This time Ken fell for actress Martha Fraser, who lived on a narrowboat on the canal. Ken had taken Eccles for a walk along the towpath when the dog jumped in the canal. Martha saved the dog's life by fishing Eccles out of the water and Ken and Martha ended up talking. He lied to Martha at first and said he was widowed, denying the existence of Deirdre back home.

Using Eccles, Ken had the perfect excuse to go wandering along the canal to see Martha in her houseboat. It didn't take long for Ken to fall for Martha. She was well read, sophisticated and arty, everything that Deirdre was not. They bonded over a shared passion for the arts and home-made leek and potato soup. Martha even bought Ken an exotic black silk kimono. When she found out he was married, she wanted to end their relationship but Ken swore his undying love.

Ken decided he would leave Deirdre and set sail with Martha. Too much of a coward to tell Deirdre he was leaving her, he wrote his goodbye in a letter he left for her to find. Peter caught Ken about to leave and made clear his contempt for his father's behaviour.

Ken walked to the canal with his suitcase in his hand, determined to leave Deirdre. Martha waited for Ken to board so they could sail off on their new life together, but at the very last minute Ken changed his mind. He stood on the bridge across the towpath as Martha sailed off on her own, and he waved her goodbye.

THE REAL WORLD
IN 2009

'King of Pop'
Michael Jackson
dies

G20 summit meets
for the first time
in London

Barack Obama
inaugurated as 44th
(and first African-
American) President
of the USA

Slumdog Millionaire
wins an Oscar

Peter tries to persuade
Ken to stay with
Deirdre and not leave
with Martha

Back home at No.1, Peter insisted that Ken should tell Deirdre the truth. **'That woman, Dad, has given you her life!'** Peter yelled at his dad.

'This is no time to exaggerate – it's a marriage of convenience, it always was!' stormed Ken.

However, Ken took Peter's comments to heart and gave Deirdre his letter to read.

'What do you want, Ken? Understanding? A round of applause?' she asked.

'Why have you shown the letter to me if it's all over? It's full of how much this Martha means to you – so much so that you were leaving me, turning your back on your family, your whole life. What made you think I'd want to read that?'

'I came back,' he said, quietly. **'I chose to be here with you.'**

'You don't realise quite how pathetic you are, do you?' snarled Deirdre. She stood up and walked to the back door, lighting a cigarette.

'Martha might be the perfect woman,' said Ken. **'But she's not you. It's you I want to spend my life with.'**

Ken pleaded with Deirdre but she wasn't in the mood for forgiveness.

'What you've done knocks me sick,' she spat. **'But there's no point going on about it because it's not going to change anything. You were too spineless to leave me. And maybe I'm exactly the same. Maybe this is it now, me and you, stuck with each other until the grave.'**

Angered by Ken's betrayal, Deirdre finally forgave him as he had forgiven her fling with Dev. However, to exact her revenge, Deirdre took great pleasure in behaving in ways she knew Ken thought were common. She sang along loudly to pop songs on the radio, watched trashy TV shows and cooked him leek and potato soup – from a tin.

GLASSES of 2009

Ken and Deirdre
make their feelings
known about Peter
and Leanne Battersby
opening a bar

The Alcoholics' Support Group

DEIRDRE, KEN AND BLANCHE DID THEIR BEST TO SUPPORT KEN'S
alcoholic son Peter when he tried to go teetotal. The Barlows trooped to the Rita
Tushingham Community Centre to join Peter at his Alcoholics' Support Group.
However, far from helping him, family grievances were aired in a most inappropriate
way. When the issue of trust was raised by the group, Ken stuck his oar in with: **'Trust.
In any family. Is vital.'**

Deirdre tutted loudly. The room turned to look at her and Ken glared at his wife.

'Deirdre, I'm trying to be honest here,' he said.

'Honesty and trust. Two things you're a world expert on, eh, Ken?'

Blanche felt she should explain to the group what was going on. Ken was morti-
fied when she started to speak.

**'Ken recently had an affair with an actress. Oh, it wasn't Nicole Kidman or
Glenda Jackson. She lived on a tugboat.'**

'It was a barge!' blurted Ken.

Peter turned to the group: **'Is it any wonder I drink?'**

Deirdre and Ken fall out again

OPENING A WINE BAR PERHAPS WASN'T THE BEST IDEA PETER BARLOW
ever had, especially as he was struggling to cope with his drinking problem. Undeterred,
he and Leanne Battersby sent in their application to open a new bar.

Ken was horrified and, using all the powers available to him, did what he could to stop Peter's licensing application being approved. Ken gave a newspaper interview slamming the Barlow family, all of them, apart from himself, of course. He divulged all about Deirdre's court case and prison stint after she fell for con man Jon Lindsay, Tracy being in prison for murder, Leanne's past as a prostitute and Peter's bigamy too.

Deirdre was absolutely furious with Ken for airing their dirty family laundry in the newspaper and the two of them fell out once again. It was Deirdre's friend Eileen Grimshaw who finally got the warring couple back together again.

E L S E W H E R E   I N   2 0 0 9

Redundancies were announced at the council and Deirdre had to reapply for her own job. It was a stressful time for her, especially when she found out that her application wasn't successful and she was out of work again.

Deirdre meets Lewis
Archer in the Rovers

2010

Deirdre and lothario Lewis

DEIRDRE CLEARLY NEEDED NEW GLASSES, BECAUSE SHE FAILED TO spot another con man about to enter her life. His name was Lewis Archer and he was tall, dark and handsome, everything that Ken was not. A suave, polite gentleman,

Deirdre and Lewis
canoodling in
the bookies

Lewis worked as an escort to accompany woman of a certain age to events around town. After Audrey's friend Claudia walked him into Weatherfield, his head was turned by the fragrant Mrs Roberts, and the two of them became romantically entwined. But Lewis was a fraud and a con man, more interested in Audrey's bank balance than her heart. Audrey wasn't happy to be courting a man who worked as an escort and Lewis promised he'd give up his work. But that's when he turned his attention to Deirdre. And Deirdre fell for him, giggling and laughing like a schoolgirl at his flattering remarks.

Deirdre invited Lewis and Audrey to a dinner party at No.1, where her stuffed marrow was the talk of the night. During dinner Deirdre flirted with Lewis, and later in the backyard Lewis and Deirdre shared a post-dinner smoke, where they flirted some more. She told Lewis she shouldn't pick on Ken since it was naughty, and Lewis replied that she was 'a very naughty girl', which made Deirdre giggle some more.

Deirdre helped Peter out by working some shifts at Barlow's Bookies, and Lewis would pop in to see her and flirt. She loved the attention but was blind to what Lewis was really up to. When Deirdre's back was turned, Lewis stamped betting slips he'd nicked and then filled to make it look like he'd won on the horses. He managed to con over £4,000 using this trick and Deirdre had no idea what was really going on. However, Peter uncovered Lewis's scam when he watched CCTV footage from the shop. It wasn't all that the camera would capture.

GLASSES of 2010

Deirdre and Lewis's kiss caught on CCTV

AT WORK IN THE BOOKIES ONE DAY, AS LEWIS FLIRTED WITH DEIRDRE, she told him she would pop home for a corkscrew so they could open a bottle of wine and have a drink together in the shop. But while Deirdre was out, Lewis nipped behind the counter to write up another fraudulent betting slip. Deirdre caught him red-handed when she returned but when she asked him what he was doing, he gave her the snog of her life to distract her. Little did they know that their kiss had been caught on CCTV – and it would be given the most public of airings.

Gail pies Deirdre

LEWIS HAD CONVINCED AUDREY TO INVEST IN A LITTLE PLACE IN GREECE where the two of them would live out their days. The Platts threw a leaving party for Audrey and Gail had a houseful of guests. But in the middle of the party, Peter stormed in to show the CCTV footage of Lewis's fraud and demanded that Audrey repay the money Lewis had 'won'. Unfortunately for Deirdre, the CCTV footage ran on to show her and Lewis snogging. The guests looked on in horror as the kiss played out from Gail's TV set to the packed room.

Deirdre and Lewis's kiss is shown at Audrey's leaving party

'Ken! Do something!'

Audrey broke down in shame, Ken was incensed and Deirdre didn't know where to look. Gail was furious with Deirdre for making a fool of her mother and she picked up the closest thing to hand – a Manchester tart filled with cream. She threw it at Deirdre and it hit her right in her face. The cream stuck to Deirdre's glasses. **'Ken! Do something!'** she wailed.

Lewis disappeared to Barbados but two years later he had the nerve to return to Weatherfield. Deirdre was so incensed when she saw him in the Rovers, she went straight over and punched him hard in the face, giving him a bloodied lip.

Ken was dismayed by Deirdre falling for Lewis, but not too surprised, not after everything they had been through. He'd seen her make a fool of herself over another fella once or twice before and now she'd done it again. In the fall-out from Deirdre lusting after Lewis, Ken and Deirdre stopped speaking and Ken was banished to the spare room.

One day Ken came into the house looking for something to eat. Deirdre was already eating her meal at the table. She deliberately hadn't cooked him anything as they were still at odds with each other. With not a word being spoken between them, Ken glanced at Deirdre eating her meal and assumed that his dinner must be in the oven. He opened the oven, but there was nothing there. He opened the fridge to see if there was anything in there but there wasn't. Neither was there anything in the cupboard for him to cook and no bread in the bread bin. Silently, Ken stood in the kitchen wondering what to do when he saw Deirdre stand up from the table with half her meal left on her plate. She walked to the kitchen bin, opened it and tipped in the remains of her dinner right in front of Ken as he looked on. Oh, those two knew how to wind each other up all right.

Deirdre's mum Blanche dies

BLANCHE'S FRIEND MAY PENN FROM PORTUGAL ARRIVED TO BREAK THE bad news to Deirdre and Ken that Blanche had passed away. Blanche had been staying with May and she explained how happy Blanche was before she died. She'd even found herself a man called Arnold who'd proposed marriage, and Blanche had accepted. The way May described Blanche painted her in a very different light to the acid-tongued battleaxe the Barlows knew. Bewildered, Deirdre wondered if May was talking about the same person.

'**With the sun on her specs and the breeze in her slacks, she was a different person, Dee Dee,**' May replied.

May Penn arrives
with sad news for
Deirdre and Ken

Deirdre is stunned by the news of Blanche's death

Deirdre was in tears when she and Ken set off for Portugal to bring Blanche's body home – and have a word with Arnold while they were there. Organising her funeral, Ken found an envelope from Blanche marked: 'Open in the event of my death.' Deirdre opened the letter and read Blanche's instructions for making her funeral the best it could be. Blanche's wish list included a pipe band and all manner of bizarre and wonderful things. Fortunately for Deirdre, there was a second list with cheaper options. She thought of everything did Blanche.

Blanche's funeral

MAY PENN LED THE DELEGATION FROM THE ONE O'CLOCK CLUB, WHO arrived with high hopes of a good day out with their flasks of hot tea. Ken and Peter were among the pallbearers and Blanche's ex-boyfriend Archie Shuttleworth was on duty as undertaker. Deirdre, upset and in tears, was offered a valium by Audrey but she declined it, saying she needed to have her wits about her. At the church, Deirdre dedicated a speech to her mum as the Andrews Sisters on CD sang the old song 'Accentuate the Positive'.

Tracy is given permission to leave prison to attend Blanche's funeral

In the cemetery, a familiar figure arrived. Tracy had been given special permission to leave jail to attend her gran's funeral. Deirdre was overjoyed that Tracy turned up but Steve was horrified to see her again. He turned to Audrey: **'Did I hear you say summat about a valium?'**

When Blanche's coffin was lowered into the ground, Deirdre placed yellow freesias at her graveside. The wake was held at the Rovers and Blanche's cronies from the One O'Clock Club helped themselves to free food, which they stuffed into their handbags. Blanche would have been proud. And finally, Ken proposed a toast and everyone raised their glasses: **'To Blanche.'**

Blanche's will reading — everybody is shocked to discover that Blanche left all her money to Tracy

Tracy released from prison

WHILE TRACY WAS IN PRISON SHE ENDED UP SHARING A CELL WITH Gail McIntyre. Gail had been sentenced for the murder of her husband, Joe. Although Gail was innocent, Tracy struck a deal with two policemen working on Gail's case. They told Tracy that if she could get a confession out of Gail, she'd be moved to an open prison. And so Tracy lied to the cops, and in court, saying that Gail had confessed to her about Joe's murder. Fortunately the jury saw through Tracy's lies and Gail was found not guilty.

When Gail was released from prison, she gave Deirdre a piece of her mind about her daughter's evil ways. Gail had been shocked by Tracy's lies in court, but she was horrified when Deirdre admitted she had known about her daughter's deceit.

Gail had further cause for concern when Tracy was released from prison later that year. Tracy's fifteen-year sentence for murder was cut short when the forensics expert who gave evidence at her trial was exposed as a fraud. With Tracy back home she caused mayhem winding up Gail and the other residents. Deirdre had to bite her tongue, secretly delighted to have her daughter back.

STREET PEOPLE

Gail McIntyre

Ken was delighted
when he discovered he
had another son

Barlow boys return

DEIRDRE DID HER BEST TO SUPPORT KEN AS HE STRUGGLED TO COPE
with the enormity of gaining another son and a grandson. Ken's past caught up with
him when a letter from an old girlfriend, Susan Cunningham, turned up behind Emily's
skirting board. Susan's letter to Ken told him he had a son, Lawrence. The news shook
Ken's world and he soon met Lawrence, and his son James.

Deirdre starts work at the medical centre

DEIRDRE STARTED WORK AS RECEPTIONIST AT THE MEDICAL CENTRE.
She took over from Gail when Gail was fired for breaching patient confidentiality.
However, subtlety and confidentiality weren't Deirdre's strong points either. When – in
2013 — Hayley turned up for her pancreatic cancer test results, Deirdre ended up
making her more worried than she already was. Hayley arrived afraid she was late for
her appointment but Deirdre reassured her she'd arrived spot on time.

'I wish some of our other patients were that punctual,' said Deirdre. 'Oh ... I
shouldn't have said that. Patient confidentiality. We only had a refresher work-
shop on it last week.'

Hayley replied that she had just popped in to pick up some results and she wasn't
sure if she needed to see the doctor or not.

A worried look crossed Deirdre's face: 'Oh no ... there is a note here that says
she does want to see you. I'm sure it's nothing to worry about. Oh! I shouldn't
have said that either. I'm not supposed to over-reassure the patients just in case
I tell them it's fine and it turns out it's something really serious and then they sue
us. Anyway, take a seat, Hayley, we're running a bit late. It's a new doctor. Not
a patch on Dr Carter, if you ask me.'

ELSEWHERE IN 2010

When mouse droppings were found at No.1, Deirdre scuttled around scared before she put elastic
bands around the bottom of her trousers to stop the mice running up her trouser legs. Ken laid
traps and poison, which was much less fun.

THINGS PEOPLE SAY

Deirdre *to* **Blanche**:
on a girls' night out when Deirdre flirts with the waiter:

'Ooh, if I was ten years younger.'

Blanche:

'You'd still be old enough to be his mother. Deirdre's already done the younger waiter thing, thank you. Not an experience I'm sure any of us want to repeat. Called Deirdre Rachid at one point. You can imagine what the One O'Clock Club made of that.'

Deirdre *sips her red wine.*

Blanche:

'Would you like me to wheel in another barrel of that stuff for you?'

Deirdre:

'Is it any wonder I drink?'

Blanche *to* **Deirdre**:

'You can be pig-headed Deirdre Hunt-as-was, sometimes, do you know that?'

Deirdre:

'Well I wonder where I get that from?'

Blanche *to* **Deirdre**
when she discovers Tracy pregnant and Peter a bigamist:

'It's a good job I'm back. What with Peter dashing about marrying women and having secret babies and Tracy landing herself in trouble. Honestly, Deirdre, have you no control over your family?'

Deirdre
when Blanche moaned she missed Carla and Tony's wedding:

'I'll tell you what mother, I've got a drop of white wine in the fridge. I'll put a fizzy aspirin in it, you can put a big hat on and pretend you're there.'

Blanche:

'You've a mean streak in you Deirdre Barlow. I don't know where you get it from!'

Blanche
when Deirdre is accidentally called Daphne:

'She's too coarse-featured for a Daphne. Daphnes are delicate with little noses and rosebud mouths, not great big lumpy backsides.'

Blanche *to* **Tracy**
after she asked if Deirdre is alright:

'Oh, don't expect an answer from contrary Mary. She changes her mind more often than she changes her sheets. Not that that's saying much.'

Ken tells Blanche he is not a homosexual! Blanche continues to 'out' him while Deirdre looks on

Blanche
to **Deirdre**:

'Ken will only go down on one knee so many times. In fact, if you leave it much longer, he won't be able to get up again without help, so think on.'

Blanche *to* **Deirdre**:
at the dinner table:

'You're always leaving your crusts. You should be enjoying them while you've still got your own teeth!'

Blanche
to **Deirdre**:

'Is someone going to make my tea, or am I going to have to phone Help the Aged?'

Blanche
to **Deirdre**:

'Good looks are a curse. You and Ken should count yourselves very lucky.'

Deirdre
apologising for her mother's acid tongue:

'Don't mind her. She's got geriatric Tourette's.'

2011

Deirdre covers up Tracy's lies – again

DEIRDRE WAS HORRIFIED WHEN SHE FOUND TRACY COVERED IN BLOOD and knocked out cold in the backyard. Steve was standing next to Tracy with blood on his hands, but it wasn't Steve who had attacked her. Tracy lied and said Steve's fiancée Becky Granger had assaulted her, but it wasn't Becky either. The culprit was Claire Peacock, who had throttled Tracy when she'd insulted the memory of her late husband Ashley. However, Tracy publicly blamed Becky for the attack as she was jealous of her marriage to Steve – and Deirdre believed every word.

After a fling with Steve while he was separated from Becky, Tracy found out she was pregnant with twins. Steve agreed to stand by her and raise the babies and Amy as a family. However, not long into her pregnancy, Tracy miscarried both babies. Deirdre was at Tracy's bedside in hospital to console and hug her daughter as she suffered the agonies of losing her twins. Tracy told her mum that if Steve found out what had happened, he'd want nothing to do with her any more. Deirdre advised that she tell Steve the truth, sure he would do the right thing and stick with her.

Suspecting her of trying to lure Steve back, Tracy called at Becky's flat but found no sign of him. An evil plan formed in Tracy's mind and she threw herself down the full flight of stairs. Becky looked on in horror, then quickly dialled 999. Tracy told everyone that Becky had pushed her down the stairs, causing her to lose the baby twins.

Tracy threatened to commit suicide if Deirdre told anyone the truth about the real reason she'd lost the twins. And so Deirdre kept the lies to herself, protecting Tracy yet again. As she'd done so many times in the past, she backed her daughter all the way. She wouldn't let anyone say a bad word about Tracy, no matter how much evil and misery she wrought.

Steve refused to believe Becky's protestations of innocence and proposed marriage to Tracy. Deirdre pleaded with Becky, for Tracy's sake, to leave Weatherfield. Becky would leave, and in some style too – on a first-class ticket to Barbados, but not before she made a shock announcement on Steve and Tracy's wedding day.

Becky stole Tracy's medical records and at the wedding reception in the Rovers, she handed the report to Steve. Steve read it and, too late, realised the horrible truth. Becky was vindicated and Tracy was exposed as an evil, twisted liar. Becky then revealed to everyone at the Rovers that Deirdre had known the truth all the time: **'She knew. Isn't that right, Dreary? Filthy liars – they run in the family.'**

Deirdre and Ken visit Tracy in hospital

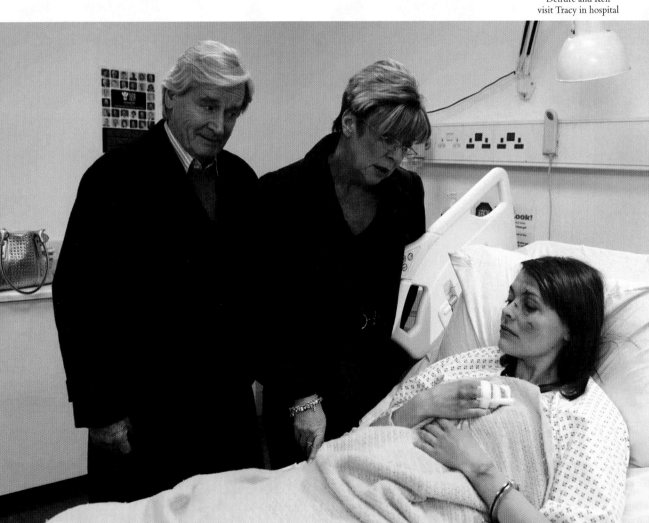

Ken is jealous of how
well Deirdre is getting
on with pottery
teacher Alex

Deirdre goes potty

DEIRDRE AND KEN DECIDED THEY NEEDED A NEW HOBBY AND JOINED A pottery class. Ken wanted to sculpt an Etruscan urn, while Deirdre chose to make an ashtray. Alex the pottery teacher praised Deirdre's attempts and upset Ken when he called him by the wrong name of Keith. Alex's attention towards Deirdre made Ken sulk in the corner of the class: **'He wouldn't know an Etruscan urn if Tracy hit him over the head with it!'**

Deirdre took her pottery throwing seriously. She told Ken that her new hobby made her feel artistic and creative. She even started reading a book on *The Treasures of Ancient Greece*. However, her talents weren't all that great. Undeterred, Deirdre was over the moon when she created a mug and couldn't wait to bring it home to drink tea from her new creation. She poured the hot tea in her mug but her face sank when the liquid drained from a hole in the bottom. Then the mug's handle dropped off and the entire mug fell onto the Barlows' dining table. **'Ken! Do something!'** she wailed.

At Ken's seventy-second birthday party, Deirdre presented him with handmade pottery gifts. Ken looked a little confused with his presents and it was left to Deirdre to explain she'd made him peanut bowls.

Ken's 72nd birthday

Ken and Deirdre's Bedtime Stories

2011 SAW KEN AND DEIRDRE STAR IN THEIR OWN SPIN-OFF SERIES. *Ken and Deirdre's Bedtime Stories* was a ten-part *Coronation Street* spin-off available online at the official ITV *Coronation Street* website, at www.itv.com/corrie.

Each webisode was three minutes long and penned by scriptwriter Jonathan Harvey. They showed Ken and Deirdre in bed together at the end of the day, discussing and bickering about the everyday life of the Barlow clan, before falling asleep.

The ten episodes were titled as follows:

1. *The One After the Wedding Blessing*
2. *The One With the Sticky Drawer*
3. *The One Where Ken Wears a Bra*
4. *The One With the Street Lamp*
5. *The One Where Ken's Had a Lot to Drink*
6. *The One With the Damp Bed*
7. *The One With the Coffee Creams*
8. *The One With the Spanner and an Egg*
9. *The One With Something in the Loft*
10. *The One Where Ken Forgets to Put the Bins Out*

Ken and his kimono
move in with Steve

2012

Ken moves out

FED UP WITH HIS WAYWARD STEPDAUGHTER AND MOANING WIFE, KEN
took to drinking in the Rovers. He chatted to Steve about Tracy, and Steve said that
if Ken ever needed to get away from Tracy and Deirdre he could always move in to
his flat, with him. And that's exactly what Ken did, just after he staggered home to tell
Deirdre and Tracy he was sick to the back teeth of them both.

In Steve's flat, Ken wafted around in his kimono and apologised to Steve for wak-
ing him up in the night: '**My bladder's not what it used to be.**' He also tidied up
Steve's kitchen, played classical musical, offered to cook lentil stew and tried to interest
Steve in his healthy eating pamphlet.

Deirdre and Julie Carp
keep an eye on Wendy
at the school fete

It was too much for Steve, and came as a relief when Deirdre and Ken made up
again and Ken moved back home to his wife.

Wendy Crozier returns

DEIRDRE'S WORLD WAS ROCKED AGAIN WHEN KEN STARTED SPENDING time with his former lover Wendy Papadopoulos. She was better known to Deirdre as Wendy Crozier, the woman who had wooed Ken when she worked for him at the *Weatherfield Recorder* many years before. Back then, Wendy's affair with Ken sent shock waves through Deirdre's world that split their marriage apart. It was fair to say that Deirdre wasn't too pleased when Wendy reappeared in their lives.

Ken stood for chair of governors at Bessie Street School and was shocked to be reunited with Wendy, who was also a school governor. Wendy told Ken she had been married since they last met, to Christos Papadopoulos, but he'd died and she was now a widow. With Ken and Wendy's friendship rekindled, they went out for a drink together and he ended up too drunk to go home. Wendy let Ken spend the night on her sofa and Deirdre was worried sick when he stayed out all night.

When Deirdre found out that Ken had spent the night with her old rival Wendy, she decided this time round she was going to fight for her man. Deirdre enlisted Rita's help, and with Rita in the driving seat of her car, the pair of them followed Ken when he went out in a taxi. **'I think Ken's up to his old tricks again!'** Deirdre told Rita. They drove off with demented Deirdre yelling at Rita to put her foot down and follow Ken's cab. **'Overtake that van!'** Deirdre yelled, to which Rita replied: **'I haven't overtaken anything in fifty years!'**

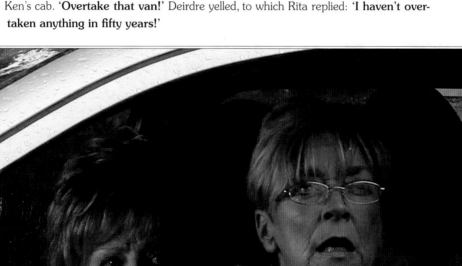

Deirdre spies
Ken kissing Wendy

Ken's taxi took him to a posh cul-de-sac in a very bay-window part of town.
Deirdre's eyes nearly dropped out of her head when she spied Ken kissing Wendy.

Deirdre's upset by
what she's just seen

Back at home, after a ciggie in the backyard, Deirdre growled at Ken, exactly as she did all those years ago when she found out about Ken's first affair with Wendy. Word for word in a repeat of what happened back then, she spat out to Ken: '**I want to know where you've been, and who with.**'

Confronted by Deirdre, Wendy admitted she wanted to try again with Ken and she lied about his night on the sofa. She told Deirdre that he'd spent the night in her bed. Ken was furious with Wendy when he found out what had happened, and he told her he didn't ever want to see her again.

After Hurricane Wendy swept out of their lives, the stormy sea of Deirdre and Ken's marriage was calm once again. They kissed and made up as Ken whispered those little words that Deirdre loved to hear: '**Cup of tea before bed?**'

Deirdre celebrated with a hot bath: '**I dropped off at one point and got my *Grazia* wet!**'

History repeats itself after Wendy returns to cause chaos for the Barlows

Deirdre warns Wendy to stay away from Ken

Deirdre finds
Tracy unconscious on
the floor at No.1

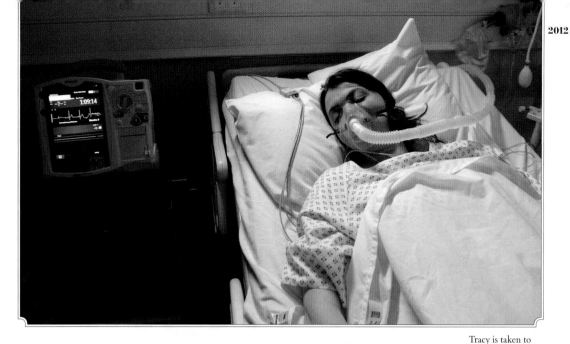

Tracy in hospital

TRACY ENDED UP IN INTENSIVE CARE IN HOSPITAL WITH A KIDNEY infection. She was desperately ill and things didn't look good. **'She could die!'** Deirdre sobbed to Ken, scared stiff she was going to lose her only child.

With Steve at her bedside, Tracy told him that he was the only reason she wanted to live, and that she'd pull through, just for him. It was a hard thing for Steve to hear, especially as he'd just got back together with girlfriend Michelle Connor. He thought it best to keep that from Tracy, for now, in her condition and all.

However, little Amy spotted her dad kissing Michelle on the street and told Grandma Deirdre. Later at the hospital, Deirdre stormed in to find Steve at Tracy's bedside, holding her hand. **'You lying toerag!'** she yelled at him as she broke the news to Tracy that Steve was seeing Michelle.

Tracy is taken to hospital where her condition worsens and she is diagnosed with a severe kidney infection

Deirdre and Ken are terrified they might lose Tracy

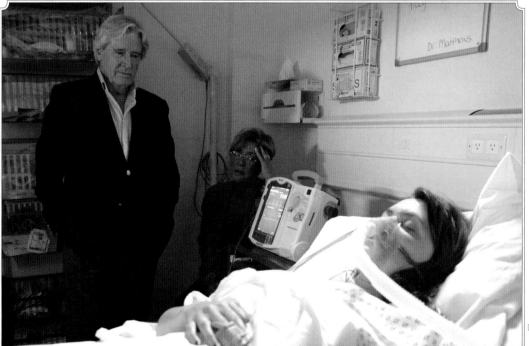

Deirdre

IN THE KITCHEN

DEIRDRE'S COOKING SKILLS WERE LEGENDARY ... FOR ALL THE WRONG REASONS.
She wasn't exactly adept in the kitchen and her long-suffering family would have to eat whatever she put in front of them. Her specialities included shop-bought chicken pie with peas and ready salted crisps. Her unusually shaped fish mould hung for years on the kitchen wall at No. 1, although we never saw her using it.

When Deirdre married Ray, she received a cookery book as a wedding gift from Rita. She wasn't an adventurous cook and would stick firmly to tried and trusted favourite dishes she'd cooked many times. She cooked first husband Ray 'steak à la something'. The steak must have gone down well, as she cooked it again when she was wooing Ken.

When she moved in with Ken and Uncle Albert, she managed to put a smile on Uncle Albert's grumpy face when she tempted him with a lamb dish he liked.

Christmas dinners were often a disaster. **'This turkey's so dry it could choke a camel,'** Blanche told her one year. She once went exotic and made her own hummus: **'I've gone all sophisticated and continental,'** she said.

One of Deirdre's successes was making *coq au vin* from scratch, which cheered Ken up no end. However, she failed miserably when she tried to pass off a Freshco chocolate cake as her own for dessert.

Deirdre's signature dishes were her stuffed marrow and traditional trifle. We are delighted to bring you her special recipes to try at home ...

Easy Trifle

1 × packet of trifle sponges (8 fingers)
Raspberry jam
2 tbsp (50ml) sherry
135g packet of strawberry jelly
225g raspberries
450ml of ready-to-pour custard (you can use 25g custard powder made up into custard if you prefer)
300ml whipping cream
Good-quality chocolate for grating
Orange for zesting

Cut the sponges in half horizontally and spread with raspberry jam. Take a large glass bowl and lay out the sponge fingers. Drizzle over the sherry.

Scatter over the raspberries.

Cut the strawberry jelly into squares, put into a mixing bowl. Boil a kettle and pour over 330ml of boiling water, stir to dissolve and then pour the liquid jelly over the fruit and sponge. Allow to cool then cover with cling film and place in the fridge to set.

When the jelly has set pour over the custard. In a separate bowl whip the cream into soft peaks and then spread over the custard.

Decorate the top with grated chocolate and a little orange zest (add a few raspberries too if you like).

Stuffed Marrow

Preheat the oven to 180°C / Gas Mark 4

1 large marrow
Olive oil
Salt and pepper

For the stuffing:
125ml olive oil
2 medium onions, finely chopped
3 ripe tomatoes, seeded and chopped
3 tbsp pine nuts

Meat version:	*Vegetarian version:*
350g minced lamb	125g basmati rice
4 tbsp finely chopped parsley	4 tbsp finely chopped parsley
salt and pepper to taste	1 tbsp finely chopped dill
	salt and pepper to taste
For the topping:	*For the topping:*
3 tbsp grated Parmesan	100g feta cheese, crumbled
4 tbsp breadcrumbs	2 tbsps Parmesan
a little fresh basil, chopped	a little fresh basil, chopped

Cut the marrow in half horizontally. Scoop out the seeds and season. For the vegetarian version, scrape out a little of the flesh (about 3 tbsps) and chop finely. Lightly oil a roasting dish and place the marrow halves in the dish.

Heat the olive oil and fry the onions. When they begin to colour add the tomatoes (and marrow flesh, for the vegetarian version). Allow to cook for five minutes. For the meat version, add the mince and cook for five minutes more. Add the pine nuts, rice, and parsley (for the vegetarian version). Stir and season to taste. Then cook very gently for ten minutes, stirring occasionally. Add a small amount of water if the rice starts to catch.

Use the stuffing to fill the marrow halves to within about a cm of the top (the stuffing will swell as the rice cooks).

Meat version:
Cover with foil and bake in the oven for 30 minutes. Take the foil off, scatter over the Parmesan and breadcrumbs, then cook for another ten minutes until golden brown. Scatter over the basil.

Vegetarian version:
Crumble over the feta, scatter over the Parmesan and then zig-zag over a bit more olive oil. Bake in the oven for about 45 minutes at the same temperature (turn the heat down if it starts to brown too much on top). Baste well with the juices. Scatter over the basil.

Serve with bread and a green salad.

BEHIND
THE
SCENES

Taking a break
while filming
Ken and Deirdre's
wedding day, 2005

Filming Ken
and Deirdre's
2005 wedding day

Anne Kirkbride
and William Roache
taking a break while
filming, 2013

Deirdre finds Rob and
Tracy rowing over him
gambling with their
joint money

2013

Tracy dates Rob Donovan

TRACY STARTED DATING CARLA'S BROTHER, ROB DONOVAN. DEIRDRE
didn't like Rob at first, not one bit, and she wondered what he was up to. But Tracy
seemed happy and that was enough for Deirdre to turn a blind eye to Rob's wrongdoings at first. However, she was right to be wary about Rob, he was a bad 'un through
and through. Deirdre nicknamed him 'Flash Harry', and Ken wasn't keen on Rob's
wide-boy ways either. **'You know who he reminds me of?'** Ken whispered to Peter,
out of earshot of Deirdre. **'Mike Baldwin!'**

Deirdre in court again

MILD-MANNERED GARAGE MECHANIC TYRONE DOBBS WAS BEATEN BY
his evil girlfriend, Kirsty Soames, over weeks and months without anyone finding
out what she was up to. Twisted Kirsty lied to the police, claiming that Tyrone had
assaulted her, and the case ended up in court. Tyrone's friends and neighbours had all
fallen for Kirsty's lies. Tyrone had to bite his tongue when he heard people who had
known him for years, including Deirdre, give evidence against him.

STREET PEOPLE

Tyrone Dobbs

Gullible Deirdre
believes Kirsty's lies
about Tyrone
beating her up

In court, Deirdre was questioned in the witness box. She said she had been walking Eccles in the ginnel when she heard Kirsty cry. She was certain that Tyrone was beating Kirsty up. '**It was so nasty, so unlike Tyrone**,' Deirdre told the court. '**You think you've got the measure of somebody … I rang Dr Carter. I'm in the medical profession and you can't risk it with the head. Kirsty said she'd fallen over and caught it on a plant pot but I had a funny feeling about it. I said to Ken later, "I've got a funny feeling about it."**'

In the gallery, Fiz Stape was furious with Deirdre for believing Kirsty's lies and condemning Tyrone. She turned to Hayley and said: '**I wanna smash her stupid glasses!**'

Head of the House of Barlow

GLASSES of 2013

DEIRDRE WAS LEFT IN CHARGE AT NO.1 WHEN KEN WENT TO CANADA to look after his grandson Adam. Adam had taken ill after collapsing at work, and as he had no other family in Canada Ken rushed to be at his side.

During Ken's absence, Deirdre was the one to whom family members turned

Outside the Rovers, David Platt taunts Peter, daring him to hit him. Peter gets a cut to the eye as Deirdre watches on in horror

for guidance and help, much more than they had done in the past. When Peter and girlfriend Carla argued and fell out, Deirdre bonded with Carla over a glass of red wine. She offered Carla some neutral advice about Peter. **'Just think of me as Switzerland in glasses,'** she said.

Deirdre did her best to make her mark as head of the family while Ken was away. She found herself rudderless at first but it didn't take her long to become firmly in charge, even if Tracy continued to stretch her patience to its limit.

Tracy tried to guilt-trip her mum into taking Amy to school while she went out with Rob, but Deirdre stood firm and said to Amy: **'Amy, this is Tracy. You may not remember her but she's your mother.'**

'I know,' Amy sighed. **'Are you two fighting? Again?'**

Tracy replied: **'Yeah, we are, Amy, but that's what we do. I'm really sorry, but your grandma can't take you to school today because she's got a really important date in the backyard with a coffee and a packet of fags.'**

Tracy tells Deirdre that Eccles should be put down for biting Amy

Deirdre finds Roy on Red Rec

DEIRDRE WAS OUT WALKING ECCLES ON RED REC ONE NIGHT WHEN SHE found Roy sleepwalking. He'd received shock news that his dad had died and, in his grief, Roy had started sleepwalking. It was Deirdre who found him walking around in the night air wearing only his pyjamas and dressing gown. Deirdre walked up to him and gently woke him and took him back to No.1 to ensure he was all right. Back at the house, Roy refused Deirdre's offer of a brandy. She mused how odd it was that she had found him in a coma-like state out on the Red Rec.

'Me and Eccles, we never know what we're going to bump into next. So when I saw you I just thought, "Ooh, watch out, Deirdre, it's another one of them weirdos, avoid eye contact" – until you got closer and then I thought, "Oh no, I know this one!"'

As Roy had once looked out for Deirdre when she went through a breakdown after Samir's death, this time Deirdre looked after Roy. She escorted him back to the cafe safe and sound.

E L S E W H E R E   I N   2 0 1 3

Deirdre tried out a spot of cold-calling for Budgen's Bathrooms, showing Tracy how it should be done. She gave Tracy a few tips on telesales, advising that a bit of razzle-dazzle would make all the difference over the phone. Deirdre told Tracy that she used that kind of talk with the patients at the medical centre. **'Words like "verruca" and "prolapsed" aren't exactly poetry but if you give it a bit of razzamatazz it'll make all the difference,'** Deirdre explained. **'It's not what you say, it's how you say it.'**

Deirdre took the telephone from Tracy and demonstrated her telephone sales technique to her daughter. She dialled the next sales prospect from Tracy's list and Tracy listened in as her mum gave her sales spiel over the phone. Using her poshest phone voice, Deirdre began: **'Good afternoon. Are you happy with the smallest room in your house? No, not the coal hole … the lavvy, the toilet. The bathroom. It's often said that the kitchen is the heart of the home, but is that true? Not everyone cooks, but we all use the bathroom.'**

Deirdre covered up the mouthpiece and whispered to Tracy: **'He's just said, "You can't boil an egg in a bidet,"'** and then she went back to her caller, who by now had recognised her voice. **'Hello? Yes it is!'** she said, before telling Tracy, **'It's Mr Chakaborti, one of our patients from the surgery!'** Tracy rolled her eyes as Deirdre carried on with the sales call, which had now turned into a flirt over the phone. **'I know … it's a small world but you wouldn't want to hoover it, as my mother used to say!'** There was a silence and then Deirdre laughed down the phone to Mr Chakaborti. **'Hey, I've told you, I'm a married woman!'**

2014

Rob Donovan moves into No.1

ROB DONOVAN'S CHARM STARTED TO WORK ITS MAGIC ON DEIRDRE. He cooked breakfast for her at No.1, swanned around the house in just his pants and called her 'Dee'. Her gut feelings about Rob were that he was a chancer and a bad 'un but he slowly won her round while Ken was away. Tracy wanted him to move in to No.1. Deirdre was dead against it. She didn't like him that much!

Deirdre plays the peace-keeper between Rob and Tracy

Tracy admits she sold
Uncle Albert's WW1
medal to fund her
wedding to Rob

Tracy devised an evil plan to get her mum to relent to Rob moving in with them. She and Rob staged a break-in at the Barlows', smashing Deirdre's handmade ceramic pot to the ground and trashing the Christmas tree. Deirdre was shocked and appalled when she saw the mess that the 'burglars' had made. But Deirdre suspected immediately it was Rob and Tracy who'd staged the robbery. She let Rob move in anyway, just to keep Tracy happy.

Rob, Tracy and Amy all sat down to dinner one night with Deirdre. Over a tuna bake that Deirdre had cooked, Amy told Rob what she'd overheard Deirdre say earlier: **'Gran says you should be neutered.'**

Deirdre put up with Rob living in her house, for Tracy's sake, but she got the shock of her life when Tracy announced that Rob had proposed. **'Engaged?'** shrieked Deirdre.

'Yeah, like a public toilet,' replied Tracy.

Later in the Rovers, Deirdre mused on whether she could carry off the colour puce at Tracy's wedding. Tracy wasn't listening to her mum – she was too busy ogling Rob's bum when he was standing at the bar. **'You can't marry a bum though, Tracy,'** Deirdre warned her daughter. **'Take it from one who's tried. Several times. Samir's was like two space hoppers in a holdall.'**

Weatherfield Women's Action Group

WHEN KEN CALLED TO SAY HE WAS STAYING IN CANADA LONGER THAN planned, Deirdre had even more time on her hands. She joined the Weatherfield Women's Action Group and took a packet of custard creams along to her first meeting.

Peter released from rehab

PETER WAS RELEASED FROM REHAB AND DEIRDRE WENT TO GREET HIM and to see how he was. Her first words on seeing sober Peter after he'd been treated for his drink problem were: **'Ooh, you look dreadful!'** Deirdre's sympathy for Peter was cut short when her attention was caught by a plate of biscuits: **'Ooh, look! Jammie Dodgers!'**

Tina McIntyre's murder

DEIRDRE'S SYMPATHY FOR PETER WOULD BE TESTED WHEN HE WAS arrested on suspicion of murdering barmaid Tina McIntyre. The real murderer was Rob, who pointed the finger of blame firmly at Peter. Things didn't look good for Peter when his affair with Tina was exposed, and Deirdre's loyalties were pulled between supporting Ken's son Peter or Tracy's fiancée Rob, who hated Peter for cheating on his sister Carla.

Deirdre tried to cope with Tina's murder and Peter's arrest all on her own. She didn't call Ken in Canada to tell him because she was frightened of what his reaction would be.

It was Eccles who sniffed out the evidence that would get Peter charged with murder. Eccles found a bracelet in the Barlows' backyard. It was the bracelet that Rob stole from Tina's flat on the night he killed her. But when Peter inadvertently handled it in No.1, he left incriminating fingerprints all over it.

Ken returns

WHEN KEN RETURNED FROM Canada, it was Carla who told him that Peter was in prison on remand. Carla filled Ken in on all the news about Peter's affair with Tina and his arrest for her murder.

To say Ken was shocked is something of an understatement. He was absolutely furious that Deirdre had kept the news from him while he'd been away.

Ken had been away for months, yet instead of a joyful family reunion, he had Deirdre in tears within minutes of walking through the front door. **'How could you not tell me?!'** Ken roared at his wife.

Ken took on Peter's cause, sure of his son's innocence. He found him a new solicitor and set out to get Peter freed.

Holiday to Wales

KEN APOLOGISED TO DEIRDRE FOR LOSING HIS TEMPER WITH HER AND as a peace offering, he planned a holiday for them both.

When Deirdre said she wanted to go somewhere warm and sunny, Rob suggested Morocco. **'Oh! Don't mention Morocco to Ken!'** she replied. **'Since I married Samir, he won't eat couscous and refuses to have dates in the house at Christmas.'**

However, their holiday wasn't to anywhere as exotic as Morocco. Ken booked a caravan trip to north Wales and he was in his element. Deirdre was distinctly underwhelmed and called it a holiday from hell.

Deirdre is
underwhelmed by her
holiday to Wales

Deirdre gets a trifle upset

DEIRDRE WAS WORRIED SICK ABOUT PETER'S MURDER TRIAL. IT WAS all she could think about. She decided to take the family's minds off the trial and offered to cook a nice meal for tea.

'**And how about your signature trifle for afters?**' asked Ken.

'**Go on then,**' smiled Deirdre, slightly cheered.

FROM SCRIPT TO SCREEN

Ken and Deirdre, Rob, Tracy and Carla have just eaten Deirdre's special meal that she's cooked …

CORONATION STREET   EP#8486   TX:08/10/2014

KEN, ROB AND TRACY SIT ROUND THE TABLE, STRAINED, WHILE DEIRDRE LOOKS FRANTICALLY IN CUPBOARDS.

DEIRDRE
I can't find the hundreds and thousands.

KEN
I'm sure it'll be fine without them.

DEIRDRE
No it won't!

SHE SLAMS A CUPBOARD DOOR SHUT AND LOOKS IN ANOTHER.

TRACY
(starts to rise)
I'll help you look.

DEIRDRE
Sit down!

TRACY SITS. THEY ALL EXCHANGE A LOOK.
CARLA COMES BACK DOWNSTAIRS AND JOINS THEM AT THE TABLE, SLIGHTLY EMBARRASSED.

ROB
(to CARLA)
All right?

CARLA NODS.

TRACY
Oh well, at least she's OK. Don't worry about our Peter.

CARLA
I'm sorry?

TRACY
Look, Peter may have killed Tina. But that doesn't mean you have to blank him.

CARLA GIVES ROB AN INCREDULOUS LOOK.

ROB
Drop it, Trace.

TRACY
It's like denying a dying man his last request, isn't it? I mean, she could have at least spoken to him.

DEIRDRE BANGS ANOTHER CUPBOARD DOOR.
KEN GLANCES OVER, WORRIED.

KEN
(hisses)
Tracy! We're not suppose to mention the P-word, remember?

TRACY
It was the T-word actually. And she started it.

CARLA
It wasn't my fault he rang!
(to ROB)
What's the T-word anyway?

ROB
Trial.

KEN LOOKS DAGGERS AT HIM

ROB
Sorry.

Deirdre's final scene

TRACY CLEANED UP THE TRIFLE FROM THE WALL AS KEN AND DEIRDRE sat on the sofa. Ken put his arm around Deirdre and told her: '**I think you need to get away for a while. Just until all this is over. Why don't you ring Bev, see if you can stay?**' Deirdre was determined not to leave, and said she needed to be at the trial. Ken managed to convince her that a break would do her the world of good.

'**But what about you?**' she asked Ken.

'**I'll be fine,**' he said. '**Besides, if I don't have to worry about you, I'll be able to focus more on Peter.**'

Reluctantly, Deirdre agreed. Her last words to Ken, and her last words on *Coronation Street*, were: '**All right. I'll ring her.**'

DEIRDRE
It's no good. We'll just have to manage
without.

SHE PICKS UP THE BOWL OF TRIFLE AND CARRIES IT TO THE
TABLE WHERE SHE PLONKS IT DOWN, UPSET.

KEN
It looks lovely.

TRACY
(to Carla)
A few lousy words. It would've cost you nowt.

CARLA
If I don't want to speak to him, I don't have
to. I don't know what it's got to do with you
anyway.

TRACY
Er, he's my brother.

DEIRDRE
(staring at the trifle)
The jelly hasn't set.

CARLA
Then you speak to him. While you're at it, you
can give him a few tips on how to get off.

KEN
(to Deirdre, quickly)
I'm sure it has.

TRACY
You cheeky cow!

ROB
Look, can we all please just calm —

DEIRDRE
It hasn't. Look!

SHE GRABS A LADLEFUL OF TRIFLE AND TILTS IT, LETTING THE
TRIFLE TRICKLE OFF AS

TRACY
Well, it doesn't matter!

DEIRDRE
(flinging the ladle down)
Yes, it does! Jelly shouldn't run! It should
wobble!

SHE SUDDENLY PICKS UP THE BOWL AND HURLS IT AT THE WALL.
THERE'S A SHOCKED SILENCE. THEN DEIRDRE HURRIES OUT OF
THE BACK DOOR, GRABBING HER CIGS AS SHE GOES.

KEN
Deirdre!
(he hurries after her.)

TRACY
(to Carla)
Well, thanks for that.

ROB
Don't blame her!

CARLA
(getting up)
I'll go.

SHE GRABS HER BAG AND HURRIES OUT. ROB GLARES AT TRACY
AND FOLLOWS.

TRACY
Oh, that's right, choose her over my mum!

2015

Farewell to Deirdre

DEIRDRE'S RETURN WAS PLANNED FOR HER 60TH BIRTHDAY ON 8 JULY 2015 and Bev was driving her home. On the day of Deirdre's birthday, there was an air of excitement at No.1 as Ken and Tracy prepared for the return of the woman they had missed so much. A surprise party had been planned to celebrate too.

Along with Ken and Tracy, Audrey was at No.1, doing Tracy's hair. Everyone was excited about Deirdre's return and wanted to look their best. Ken had even put on a tie and looked very dapper indeed.

When the doorbell rang, Ken went to answer it, expecting it to be Liz calling round for the cake they'd arranged for the party. But it wasn't Liz, it was Bev at the door …

FROM SCRIPT TO SCREEN:

CORONATION STREET   EP#8678   TX:08/07/2015

> KEN
> Bev! You're early!'
>
> *SHE IS LOOKING UPSET. HE LOOKS OUT TO THE CAR.*
>
> KEN
> Where is she?
>
> *BEV COMES IN.*
>
> BEV
> I'm so sorry, Ken.
>
> KEN
> Is she not with you?
>
> BEV
> I need a word.
>
> *BEV GOES THROUGH TO THE LIVING ROOM. SHE CLOCKS AUDREY. THEY HAVE A SECOND OF AWKWARDNESS.*
>
> BEV
> Oh hello.
>
> AUDREY
> Hi, Bev. Everything all right?
>
> TRACY
> Where's Mam?
>
> BEV
> I'm so sorry. I've got some terrible news.
>
> *SHE TRIES NOT TO CRY.*
>
> KEN
> What on earth has happened?
>
> BEV
> There's no easy way to say this but Deirdre died this afternoon.

> *KEN AND THE OTHERS ARE FLOORED BY THIS INFORMATION. SILENCE DESCENDS. KEN LOOKS STUNNED.*
>
> *KEN SITS IN HIS CHAIR, STUNNED. TRACY IS BEWILDERED. BEV IS STANDING. AUDREY COMES THROUGH FROM THE KITCHEN WITH A BRANDY FOR HER. THEY SHARE AN AWKWARD SMILE.*
>
> AUDREY
> There you go, Bev.
>
> BEV
> Thank you.
>
> KEN
> I don't understand it. I only spoke to her yesterday.
>
> *TRACY SHAKES HER HEAD.*
>
> TRACY
> She can't be dead. I mean, how did it happen? You can't be there one minute and not the next.
>
> BEV
> I found her. I was going to phone but I thought it was best done face to face. I've tried to keep it together but ...
>
> *SHE SITS AND CRIES. THE OTHERS ALL SIT THERE IN STUNNED SILENCE. THEIR SHOCK IS PALPABLE.*
>
> *THE OTHERS LISTEN ON AS BEV ATTEMPTS TO TELL THEM HOW DEIRDRE DIED.*
>
> BEV
> She was so looking forward to coming back.
>
> TRACY
> Was she?

BEV

Up with the lark this morning. I could hear her
singing in the shower. It was such a lovely day.
I don't know if she'd sussed about the party but
she kept giggling about ... about you fussing, Ken.

KEN FINDS A HALF-SMILE.

BEV

How she had to be back. Six on the dot. Or her
life wouldn't be worth living. We had muesli for
breakfast. I've got this shop near me does nice
muesli. She'd bought a box to bring back.

KEN

She's never really been one for muesli.

TRACY

No.

KEN

She likes an egg.

TRACY

Egg in a cup.

BEV

She'd packed all her stuff yesterday. Couldn't
wait to load the car up. We loaded it this morning.
Listened to Ken Bruce. I'd not much in for lunch so
I warmed some soup up. After, she said she fancied
a sit in the garden. I decided to phone my cousin
and afterwards I went into the garden. She was
sat on a patio chair. I thought she was asleep.
She looked so peaceful. I don't think she suffered.
She can't have.

TRACY PUTS HER HEAD IN HER HEADS AND SOBS VIOLENTLY.

AUDREY

Oh, Tracy.

KEN GETS UP AND GOES TOWARDS TRACY. SHE GETS UP AND THEY HUG.

BEV

I said her name. Then again. And I just knew.

BEV

I tried waking her. And then I called the
ambulance. It was like she'd gone to sleep and not
woken up.

KEN

Where is she?

BEV

Paramedics have taken her to the hospital.
They obviously couldn't be sure but well the bloke
felt she'd probably had an aneurism. He said she
wouldn't have suffered.

TRACY IS CRYING.

BEV

She didn't look like she'd suffered.

AUDREY MOVES AND COMFORTS TRACY, WHO CRIES ON HER SHOULDER.

BEV

I almost forgot.

*SHE OPENS HER BAG. PULLS OUT DEIRDRE'S GLASSES WRAPPED IN
A PAPER NAPKIN.*

BEV

I didn't know what to do with them.

*SHE HANDS THEM TO KEN. HE STARES A MOMENT BEFORE TAKING THEM.
HE RUSHES INTO THE KITCHEN, HOLDING THE GLASSES. HE STEADIES
HIMSELF AGAINST THE WORK SURFACE AND TRIES NOT TO CRY.*

The Weatherfield Gazette

Death Notices

✝

BARLOW, DEIRDRE ANN

(*née* HUNT, *was* LANGTON, *previously* RACHID)

8 July 1955 ~ 8 July 2015

Passed away suddenly and peacefully on her sixtieth birthday. Much-loved only daughter of the late Blanche and Donald Hunt, loving wife of Ken; loving mother to Tracy; caring grandmother to Amy and Simon; stepmother to Peter; a good friend to many. Will always be missed. Remembered with love in the hearts of family, friends and millions of *Coronation Street* fans all over the world.

THINGS PEOPLE SAY

Blanche
to **Deirdre**:

'Take time with your daughter, Deirdre. Precious time.'

Blanche
to **Deirdre**:

'Cometh the hour, Deirdre, cometh the woman. Cometh Blanche Hunt.'

Blanche
to **Deirdre**:

'You don't half know how to embarass people, don't you? You've been embarassing me all your life.'

Blanche
to **Deirdre**:

'Fancy finding out your fella's gone off with some floozy on a boat. Adds a whole new meaning to messing about on the water.'

Deirdre
to **Blanche**:

'I am so stupid.'
Blanche:
'It's taken you fifty-odd years to realise that? Oh, Hallelujah!'

Deirdre
explaining to **Eileen** *that when she dies her whole life will be summed up as ...*

'Disappointed.'
Eileen:
'With an undercurrent of fear.'

Deirdre and Anne's
AWARDS

The 2000 cast
in celebratory mood

TV Times Awards 1983

TV Personalities of the Year:
William Roache, **Johnny Briggs** and **Anne Kirkbride**

Oracle TV poll 1990

Best Actress:
Anne Kirkbride

TV Quick Awards 1998

Best Soap Storyline:
Deirdre's imprisonment

TV Quick Awards 1998

Most Dramatic Storyline:
The jailing of Deirdre

British Soap Awards 2015

Outstanding Achievement:
Anne Kirkbride

1972	1973	1974	1975	1976	1977	1978	1979	1980
1	32	67	70	62	62	59	50	58

1990	1991	1992	1993	1994	1995	1996
118	91	76	100	63	63	94

2004	2005	2006	2007	2008	2009
111	116	108	103	78	89

Deirdre's

VITAL STATISTICS

1981	1982	1983	1984	1985	1986	1987	1988	1989
70	55	75	69	78	51	63	61	69

1997	1998	1999	2000	2001	2002	2003
112	86	102	96	83	97	108

2010	2011	2012	2013	2014	2015
99	92	94	51	72	0

DEIRDRE APPEARED IN OVER 3,300 EPISODES OF *CORONATION STREET*. For a staggering 40 years she would grace our screens almost weekly. Episode counts given above are the official stats according to Corriepedia – the online fan-compiled repository of all things *Corrie*.

Anne Kirkbride with
the waxwork of Deirdre
Barlow at Madame
Tussauds, Blackpool

How well
DO YOU KNOW DEIRDRE?

ALL THE ANSWERS CAN BE FOUND SOMEWHERE IN THE BOOK
(and at the bottom of the page).

1. **In what year was Deirdre's character introduced to *Coronation Street*?**

   a: 1972
   b: 1974
   c: 1976

2. **What item is most associated with Deirdre?**

   a: Glasses
   b: Slippers
   c: Gloves

3. **How many step-grandsons does Deirdre have – and can you name them?**

   a: Three
   b: Two
   c: Five

4. **Where in Morocco did Deirdre go on holiday when she met her toy-boy Samir?**

   a: Agadir
   b: Rabat
   c: Casablanca

5. **Which of these night classes did Deirdre attend?**

   a: Creative writing
   b: Pottery throwing
   c: Life drawing

6. **Which musical instrument did Deirdre play in the Rovers Return?**

   a: Harmonica
   b: Ukulele
   c: Piano

7. **In what year did Deirdre marry Ken for the second time?**

   a: 2005
   b: 2001
   c: 2000

8. **Where did Deirdre work for most of her time in *Coronation Street*?**

   a: The corner shop
   b: The Kabin
   c: The Rovers Return

9. **What is Deirdre's middle name?**

   a: Ann
   b: Blanche
   c: Tracy

10. **What was the name of Deirdre's dad, who died when she was a child?**

    a: Donald
    b: Robert
    c: Michael

11. **How many husbands has Deirdre had – and can you name them?**

    a: Three
    b: Four
    c: Seven

12. **Who did Deirdre stand against in her fight for the role of Weatherfield Councillor?**

    a: Alf Roberts
    b: Mike Baldwin
    c: Fred Elliott

13. **What did Deirdre say to the judge when she was sentenced to jail for fraud?**

    a: 'I didn't do any of it!'
    b: 'I'm innocent!'
    c: 'It wasn't me!'

14. **What was Deirdre's signature dish she cooked for her family?**

    a: Roast lamb
    b: Stuffed marrow
    c: Stuffed peppers

15. **And finally, complete this Deirdre quote:**
    'Jelly shouldn't run, it should ...'

    a: Set
    b: Curdle
    c: Wobble

1. 1972 2. Glasses 3. Three – Adam, Simon and James 4. Agadir 5. Pottery throwing 6. Harmonica 7. 2005 8. The corner shop 9. Ann 10. Donald 11. Three – Ray, Ken and Samir 12. Alf Roberts 13. 'I didn't do any of it!' 14. Stuffed marrow 15. Wobble

221

Sources

LIFE ON THE STREET

1972

p. 13   'I was down for an audition for something ...' D&M, 2012

p. 13   'They said: "If we like you ..."' D&M, 2001

p. 13   'That was my first *Street* scene ..."' GK, p. 36

p. 13   'My very first scene was in a pub ...' TR50, p. 96

1975

p. 24   'There had been a sort of bond ...' DL35, pp. 126–7

1978

p. 37   'The producer knocked on my door ...' D&M

p. 37   'They didn't know what ...' DL35, p. 143

1979

p. 45   'There was this lorry upside down ...' DL35, p. 145;
DL40, p. 130; DLRR, p. 62 ff

1981

p. 59   'When they put Deirdre together ...' D&M, 2012

p. 59   'It was very special ...' DL35, p. 158

1983

p. 63   'The most explosive, romantic situation ...' GK, p. 67

p. 63   'Don't be too hasty ...' GK, p. 67

p. 63   'The *Sun* asked a computer ...' GK, p. 67

p. 63   '*The Times* ran a history ...' GK, p. 67

p. 63   'I think Ken is a nice man ...' GK, p. 67

p. 63   'I rather think Ibsen ...' GK, p. 67

p. 63   'Ken and Deirdre were on ...' GK, p. 67

p. 63   'I thought the story would spark off ...' GK, p. 36

p. 66   'I wasn't prepared for it ...' DL35, p. 166

p. 66   'It's the question you get asked ...' D&M

1987

p. 76   'It was a complete departure ...' DL35, p. 187

1989

p. 83   'Deirdre confronting Ken ...' GK, p. 68.

p. 83   'Give him the boot ...' GK, p. 68

1993

p. 99   'When Anne Kirkbride had to leave ...' DL35, p. 229

1998

p. 122   'I still have trouble ...' TR50, p. 168

p. 122   'When Deirdre was finally freed ...' TR50, p. 168

2014

p. 210   Trifle scene: original ITV script

2015

p. 212   Farewell scene: original ITV script

THE DEIRDRE LOOK

p. 106   'What I do every so often is ...' D&M

Online

Corrie.net – www.corrie.net
(author's *Coronation Street* weekly updates since 1995)

Corriepedia.com –
coronationstreet.wikia.com/wiki/Corriepedia

ITV – www.itv.com/corrie

Documentary, DVD and video

Coronation Street: Golden Anniversary Collection, ITV, 2010

Coronation Street: 1970–1979, Network, 2011

Coronation Street: 1980–1989, Network, 2011

Coronation Street: 1990–1999, Network, 2011

Coronation Street: 2000–2009, Network, 2011

The Coronation Street Collection: Deirdre, ITV/Granada TV, 1995

Deirdre and Me, Granada TV/ITV, 2001

Deirdre and Me: 40 Years on Coronation Street, Shiver/ITV, 2012

Women of Coronation Street, ITV/Granada TV, 1998

Books

Graeme Kay, *Life in the Street: Coronation Street Past and Present*,
Boxtree, 1991

Daran Little, *The Coronation Street Story: Celebrating Thirty-Five
Years of the Street*, Boxtree, 1995

Daran Little, *Life and Times at the Rovers Return*, Index/Granada
Television, 1995

Daran Little, *The Women of Coronation Street*, Boxtree, 1998

Daran Little, *Forty Years of Coronation Street*, Andre Deutsch,
2000

Tim Randall, *Coronation Street Treasures*, Carlton, 2005

Tim Randall, *Fifty Years of Coronation Street*, Headline, 2010

Tim Randall, *The Rovers Return: Coronation Street Official
Companion*, Headline, 2014

Abbreviations of sources

D&M   Either *Deirdre and Me*, 2001 or *Deirdre and Me: 40 Years
on Coronation Street*, 2012

DL35   *The Coronation Street Story: Celebrating Thirty-Five Years
of the Street*

DL40   *Forty Years of Coronation Street*

DLRR   *Life and Times at the Rovers Return*

GK   *Life in the Street*

TR50   *Fifty Years of Coronation Street*

About the Author

GLENDA YOUNG IS A WRITER AND LIFELONG *CORONATION STREET* FAN.
Glenda has written updates to *Coronation Street: The Complete Saga* and *Coronation
Street: The Complete Saga: An Epic Novel of Life in 'the Street' from 1960 to the
Present Day*. She hopes one day to work for Rita and Norris as the paper girl in the Kabin.
glendayoungbooks.com

Acknowledgements

THE AUTHOR WISHES TO THANK

the cast and crew of *Coronation Street*

Barry Smith

Corriepedia

the team at the Coronation Street Blog

Shirley Patton and Sarah Hussain
at ITV Studios Global Entertainment

Ajda Vucicevic
at Penguin Random House

Kieran Roberts, Alison Sinclair, Dave Woodward,
Dominic Khouri and Helen Nugent
at Coronation Street, ITV Manchester

Mark Robinson
at Shiver TV

Deirdre's
FAMILY TREE

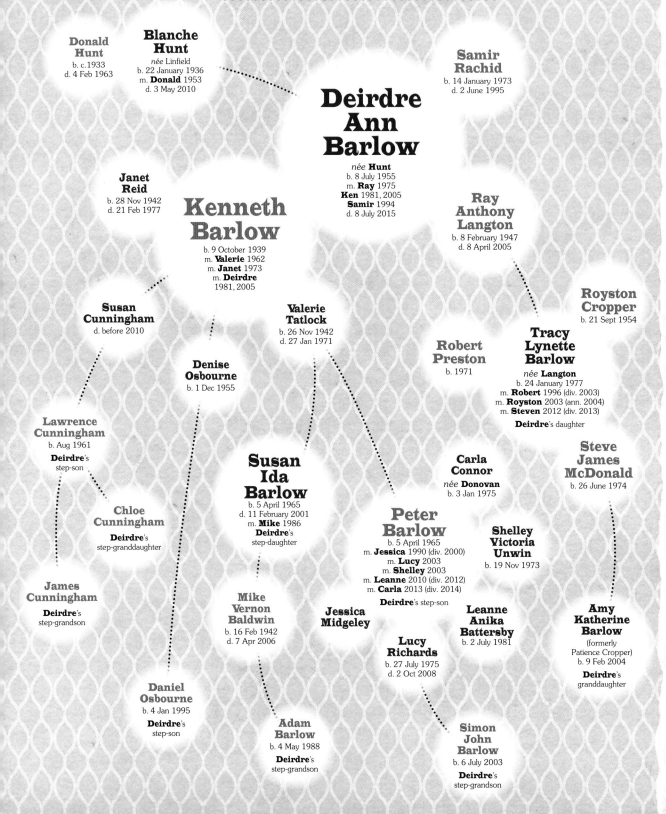

Donald Hunt
b. c.1933
d. 4 Feb 1963

Blanche Hunt
née Linfield
b. 22 January 1936
m. **Donald** 1953
d. 3 May 2010

Samir Rachid
b. 14 January 1973
d. 2 June 1995

Deirdre Ann Barlow
née **Hunt**
b. 8 July 1955
m. **Ray** 1975
Ken 1981, 2005
Samir 1994
d. 8 July 2015

Janet Reid
b. 28 Nov 1942
d. 21 Feb 1977

Kenneth Barlow
b. 9 October 1939
m. **Valerie** 1962
m. **Janet** 1973
m. **Deirdre**
1981, 2005

Ray Anthony Langton
b. 8 February 1947
d. 8 April 2005

Susan Cunningham
d. before 2010

Valerie Tatlock
b. 26 Nov 1942
d. 27 Jan 1971

Royston Cropper
b. 21 Sept 1954

Denise Osbourne
b. 1 Dec 1955

Robert Preston
b. 1971

Tracy Lynette Barlow
née **Langton**
b. 24 January 1977
m. **Robert** 1996 (div. 2003)
m. **Royston** 2003 (ann. 2004)
m. **Steven** 2012 (div. 2013)
Deirdre's daughter

Lawrence Cunningham
b. Aug 1961
Deirdre's
step-son

Susan Ida Barlow
b. 5 April 1965
d. 11 February 2001
m. **Mike** 1986
Deirdre's
step-daughter

Carla Connor
née **Donovan**
b. 3 Jan 1975

Steve James McDonald
b. 26 June 1974

Chloe Cunningham
Deirdre's
step-granddaughter

Peter Barlow
b. 5 April 1965
m. **Jessica** 1990 (div. 2000)
m. **Lucy** 2003
m. **Shelley** 2003
m. **Leanne** 2010 (div. 2012)
m. **Carla** 2013 (div. 2014)
Deirdre's step-son

Shelley Victoria Unwin
b. 19 Nov 1973

James Cunningham
Deirdre's
step-grandson

Mike Vernon Baldwin
b. 16 Feb 1942
d. 7 Apr 2006

Jessica Midgeley

Leanne Anika Battersby
b. 2 July 1981

Amy Katherine Barlow
(formerly
Patience Cropper)
b. 9 Feb 2004
Deirdre's
granddaughter

Lucy Richards
b. 27 July 1975
d. 2 Oct 2008

Daniel Osbourne
b. 4 Jan 1995
Deirdre's
step-son

Adam Barlow
b. 4 May 1988
Deirdre's
step-grandson

Simon John Barlow
b. 6 July 2003
Deirdre's
step-grandson